...es gens qui arrivent à vivre en éveil total sont considérés comme des Saints parce que de l'extérieur on peut sentir leur Joie intérieure.

La méditation est une entrée dans une forme de réel, un d'éveil total. Elle nous conduit jusqu'aux frontières de ce monde et nous rend ensuite à la vie quotidienne remplie et de solutions.

Nous vivons régulièrement des expériences psychiques plupart des gens préfèrent nier ou ignorer ces phénomènes que de changer leur propre vision du monde. Ces phénomènes comme les intuitions, les rêves, les pensées sont les premiers que nous lance le subconscient. Une intuition est une pensée intérieure. Elle se manifeste lorsque nous obtenons une information intérieure. Il faut par contre être très à l'écoute de soi, peu de gens sont capable de les détecter.

Il y a toutes sortes de moyens d'être totalement dans par des moyens spirituels comme la méditation, les autres Pensez-y: Voyez, sentez, touchez, goûtez comme si c'était la première et la dernière fois que vous étiez dans votre affrontez la peur de vous découvrir, méditer ce n'est...

Willow Moon Publishing

Cataloging Data Carle, Eveline Dancing Feat: A Dancer's Journey to 14
Golden Rules of Teaching/Eveline Carle. –1st U.S. Edition Summary: Eveline's journey through ballet school and the national ballet company, connecting with the sacredness both inside and out, so that one day she could
find herself back on a path of service, making the teaching of dance a golden
experience. Edited by Sarah Clarke Hardcover ISBN:978-1-948256-17-9,
Paperback ISBN: 978-1-948256-18-6 Typeset: Minion Pro by Jodi Stapler

Dancing Feat

A DANCER'S JOURNEY TO
14 GOLDEN RULES OF TEACHING

A memoir by Eveline Carle

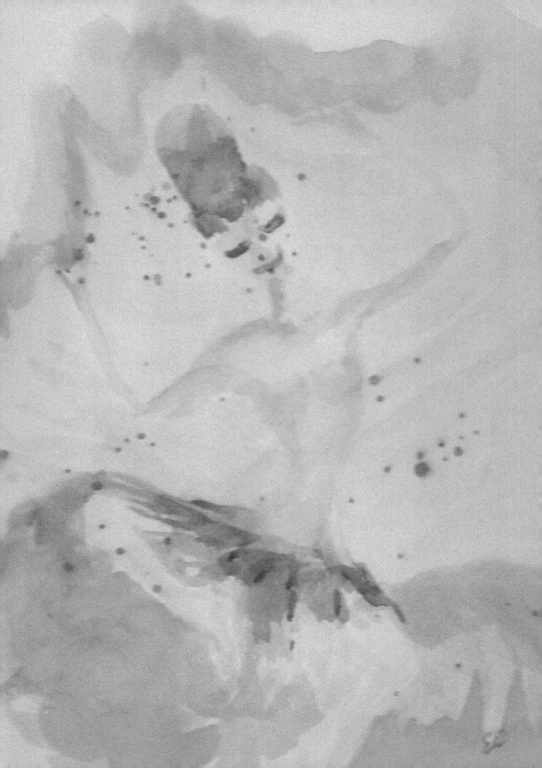

PREFACE

I decided to write my story fully aware that no one may be interested in reading it, but I needed to see what would happen if I were to tell my story as I remembered experiencing it as a child. The practice of writing gave me perspective on the path I followed that brought me to where I am now. In the process of writing I began to see how my philosophy on teaching dance had emerged, and soon, 14 golden rules came to the surface.

The study of dance was not always the sacred haven I may have wished for, but through my own struggles and my experience connecting with a sacredness both inside myself and on the dance floor, I found ways to make the learning of dance a golden experience.

I do not consider myself a special human being, but I know I have often felt alone. By telling my story as honestly as possible, I hope to reach out to others and share the practices I have found to breathe through difficulties and obstacles and connect back with others with love.

Table of Contents:

Introduction

I spent a lot of time trying to find home, whether it was a place, a state of mind, or a feeling in my heart. As I danced my way up and down the streets in various places and times, my belief was that one day, home would just appear. But it did not—not like that anyway. With time, finding home became a journey rather than an ultimate destination, a purpose rather than a goal, and a process rather than something someone would just give me. Home eventually became dance itself: my token of commitment to life.

With time, as I grew roots in this new found land inside myself, I started questioning: Where did I come from? How did I become who I am? I have spent a lot of my life running: running away from the old and towards the new. Now that I am slowing down, my past is catching up to me; it carries both wisdoms and pains. My life has changed many times and in many ways, but somehow the thought of the future is scarier than it ever was.

I want to be like a window squeaking clean because of its transparent honesty. I want to let all the walls down, let life in, and let myself out. I want to believe that I will be safe, loved, and cared for. I am afraid, however, that this inner desire to take full responsibility for who I am and who I want to be is resurrecting some of the old battles I thought remained in the past. These old battlegrounds give off a smell of the past that makes me wish I could find a way around myself.

I am 33 as I am writing this, and it is fair to say that I analyze things way too much. It is both exhilarating and time-consuming. I had a husband once, who told me that in writing, one should never use two adjectives for one thing. "Just pick the best one," he used to say. Men—they have a comforting way of asserting their opinions as the ultimate truth: comforting. Men—they also have a dogmatic way of speaking their own truth in a way that leaves no room for anybody else's: dogmatic. Here it is: comforting and dogmatic—the two adjectives.

I grew up speaking French. Learning English in my teens helped me assign new words to everything I had known forever, providing a second view of them, a new window into the world. Writing in English as a second language has helped me bypass the restraint I originally felt towards writing about my life. There was a freedom I felt when I would speak up in English that I never felt when I would speak up in French. And let's face it: swearing in a foreign language is a lot more fun. There's no guilt attached to the sin since nobody ever told me not to use English swear words growing up.

As an eternal optimist who believes in true passion, I was often convinced that with the right amount of effort and sweat, anything can be accomplished. But sometimes it's not always true. Sometimes things change, go away, fade away, or sometimes we just have to give up and turn the page. I was married and divorced twice. I separated from my second husband a year ago and decided that this time I had to love myself first. This stuff, this realization process sucks. It's real work. Being honest with myself about what was really going on took great courage. Anyone who has experienced a breakup will agree that in the midst of a split, the thought of dying is not unappealing. It breaks your soul, it breaks your convictions, and it breaks your ability to trust yourself at least for a while.

I am a classically trained ballet dancer. Dance defined me from an early age. I moved to the United States in 1999, where I started a new life, and I now own and run two dance studios on Cape Cod. Being a dance teacher to students age 3 to 103 has utilized the best and most tender parts of me.

Teaching dance is what has helped me continue on and move further ahead in my life on more than one occasion. Teaching has brought me back to life many times. It's the teaching, the relationship with each individual, and the philosophy that I hold dear behind dance education that continues to expand me and make me stronger.

As I share my 14 Golden Rules about teaching dance, I hope to open a door on the sweetness and tenderness that has deepened my dance teaching experience over the last 10 years. I truly believe we have the opportunity to build someone's self-esteem by offering them an opportunity to grow doing something they love. These golden rules go beyond dance education and could be applied to any field of life where one has the option of making a difference by being patient, loving, careful, and more importantly, themselves.

Chapter 1: Derrière la Scène [Behind the Scene]

The Catalyst

I grew up in Montréal, Canada. My mother and father were the perfect couple—smart, driven, kind, and handsome. My mom was kicking ass as a programmer analyst, and my dad was finishing his doctorate in history. They were renovating an old historical stone house on the north side of Montréal Island that had no running water or heat. They had purchased the home as a young couple and had manage to receive a grant for doing the renovation work on the house. Soon after the house was in move-in condition with hot water coursing through the pipes and the chill gone on those tough Canadian winter nights, they were ready to start a family. I was born first, then my brother Étienne, and then my brother François. We were a happy family.

I was seven when my youngest brother Francois drowned in the pool on one sunny summer day. My other brother Étienne was five at the time. My parents left Etienne and me with my godmother for the day while they were occupied with other things. Two-year-old François stayed home with the babysitter who was on the phone and left the ladder of our above ground pool out. My brother must have thought he could swim alone. He couldn't. No one was there to watch him struggle in the water as he took his last breath. It was an accident.

We live our lives accumulating things, building relationships, and securing our futures; death is not something that most of us want to think about while we're living. The fact that life can be taken away at any moment can destroy one's sense of comfort and well-being. Death, however, is hardest for the people who are left behind.

After the accident, Francois was actually kept alive at the hospital for a few weeks. He was in a coma. My godmother was the one who told my brother and me that Francois was not going to survive. She had taken us out for lunch to the barbecue chicken restaurant chain we used to go to; they had awesome kids' meals with the dessert included. As we sucked down the last bite of our desserts, she told us our little brother wouldn't be coming back. What was there to say? We were in a public place, and I didn't know how to react.

She brought us to the park afterwards across the street, but I still didn't know how to react or what to feel. It was surreal. I remember being on the swing, and I remember feeling like nothing was ever going to be the same. I was frozen. I couldn't talk. I couldn't smile. I couldn't cry. I would be right about nothing being the same. I don't think I was ever able to play with other kids after that. It was too much reality for a seven-year-old.

After Francois's death, my mom lost touch with reality. She became completely absent. My dad was not doing that much better at being there for us. He was in shock. I remember the ride back home from the hospital the night my little brother was unplugged and released into death's arms. Everyone was crying in the car, yet I wasn't. In that moment, I believed someone had to keep their head on their shoulders. It felt as though everything was collapsing, and I seriously thought I was the only hope for any kind of recovery for this family. I remember telling Étienne on the ride back, "Nobody will ever touch you. I'll take care of you." That day defines me: I was an old seven-year-old. And somehow, sometimes, I feel my heart stayed right there at seven.

My mom left our family shortly afterwards. She just couldn't take it. She just packed her stuff one day and left quietly.

My parents told me that when the babysitter called them the day of the accident, and when they returned to the house, they looked at each other before leaving for the hospital and knew their relationship had ended. My mom had lost her mother a few months prior and was questioning her own life and who she was. My brother's death had the potential of bringing them closer together or pushing them further apart. It did the latter.

Me & my little brother

The Fire

A year before François's death, my brother Étienne accidentally started a fire in the house that my parents had rebuilt. He was only four years old at the time and seemed to have developed an insatiable fondness for fire. He would find ways to play with fire at every chance he had, and this time, he found a lighter to play with, discovered a good place to hide it, and then waited to explore its magnificence. He ultimately chose the space beneath my parents' bed as the best place to fiddle with it, and it's probably easy to visualize what came next. It only took an instant for the flames to travel from the lighter to the mattress, from the mattress to the sheet, and then to the carpet.

He could have very well just roasted in with the flames himself, but miraculously, in his panic, he made it to my mom in the kitchen and whispered, rather than screamed: "Feu, feu" ("Fire, fire"). My mom paused, then realized what he was saying.

The whole house could have gone up in flames that day, but luckily, my mom and dad somehow managed to bring the burning mattress out onto the street so it wouldn't burn the rest of the house down. By that time, the smoke alarm was already going off, and I had dressed both Étienne and François, packed our clothes, my mom's slippers, and taken the money hidden on top of the fridge in case everything burned up. By the time the firefighters showed up at the house, I was standing outside with my two brothers on the sidewalk in our winter coats, holding a bag of clothes.

In a way my, mom had been preparing me for this type of survival instinct by telling me a story over and over again about a little girl who planned to leave in the middle of the night, by herself, to go live alone in a country house. Every time she told the story, the little girl in the story was me. In this tale, I packed the essential stuff—some clothes, some money, some food—then hitchhiked to our house in Saint-Jean-Sur-le-Richelieu, a little village by the Richelieu River minutes outside the city. I'm not entirely sure why the hell my mom would want to be giving me tips on the best way to flee, but maybe the story was her own fantasy, or maybe her intuition told her that I would eventually be on the road for most of my life. Maybe the story was her way of teaching me what many mothers teach their children: that you can always just pack your bags and go.

I did feel prepared that day of the fire at age six to act quickly and decisively. But I did not feel that prepared a year later after our little brother's death when I saw my mother leave.

My mom moved into a small apartment by herself downtown in the city while my brother and I stayed with our dad. We would see her for a day or two every other weekend. It was hard to see my mother go and watch her walk away from everything she had, including us. She just checked out. My brother and I would visit her, but she simply didn't know what to do with us. She refused any kind of physical closeness: she wouldn't let me touch her hands when we would walk on the street; she said they were too damped. She wouldn't let me sit close to her on the couch, as she thought my body was too warm. Étienne and I just didn't know what to do. She would disappear for stretches at a time while we were there. We would be right next to her and call her name, and she just wouldn't answer. She would get lost in herself.

There was no need for my parents to try to hide the fact that they had separated; we knew what was going on, but they never talked to us or told us anything about it. I think sometimes parents forget that the kids live in the house, too, and that we do in fact pick up on things. I know it's difficult to talk about separating from your spouse, and yes, everyone feels like an asshole, but if you don't explain what is going on, your children will imagine their own reasons for the separation. For example, I concluded that I wasn't good enough for my mother to stay. I thought, she must have loved our little brother the most because when he left, she had no reasons to stay. It would be great if we all had ironclad egos and steely self-confidence, but we don't. If parents don't explain their separation properly to their children, then the reason, the

me at the country house

children might decide, is them.

My mom wrapped herself in music. She played the piano from the time she was a young girl. She had always been an avid player and studied both mathematics and music for a long time before committing to the study and practice of mathematics. As a kid, I remember twirling around the living room when she played; her music gave birth to my love for dance. My mother's love of music, however, went from good to bad; after the accident, she became obsessed with it. All she ever wanted to do was play the piano. She started a master's degree in music at McGill University. She would play as many hours of the day as she could, and she even had a keyboard with headphones so she could play during the night without disturbing anyone while they slept. Then she started to sleep under her grand piano. It was strange.

When we visited her, she wouldn't stop playing. We were left to ourselves, my brother would act up, I was wound up, and I thought it was my duty to step in and be the mom. I figured, who else was going to do it? My mom could hardly put one foot in front of the other. My brother needed discipline, so I would beat the crap out of my brother while she played. I hate that I may have brought him more pain, but the whole thing hurt both of us so much. There is no word to describe how much I love my brother. It was just a painful situation.

I have few memories from the period of time before my little brother died; most of my memories are based on pictures in photo albums. The one thing I do remember clearly, however, was being concerned about my mom's well-being.

I have an audio cassette tape that I made for my mom for Christmas when I was just about six. In the recording, I played some pieces on the piano, I told her I loved her, and I told her I wanted to be a better daughter. I was basically pleading for her to stay with us.

That Christmas I went to a local gift store that was walking distance from my house. I picked out a musical note cast in gray ceramic that could be hung on a wall. I wanted to attach it to the tape I made and offer it to her for Christmas. I am not too sure how I ended up paying for the present, but I remember giving it to her. Even back then at such a young age, I knew my mom wasn't well.

In the next chapter I am introducing the first rule, and I believe the "rule" was developed from remembering feeling so aware of everyone and everything around me early on. I can't forget how I felt, so therefore I need to apply the fact that kids are sensitive and caring, no matter how old, in my handlings with them. As for my mother, she did get better with time. She is much more well-rounded and loving now; it just took her a while to find her path again.

me at home

Golden Rule 1

Never Assume Kids Are Dumb

These experiences from my early childhood gave me something that I use to this day in teaching dance. Simply put, we should never assume a child is dumb.

I was very aware as a young child what was going on in my home. I didn't want anyone to try to hide it from me, I wanted to be kept in the loop, and I wanted to be involved. When I teach kids today, I am aware that they are sensitive beings who respond positively or negatively to our actions, words, and states of mind. Children pay attention to the way we interact with them and respond to us accordingly. When it comes to teaching kids, sincerity and honesty go a long way.

As a child, I wanted to understand a lot of things—everything. With time, I realized that the hardship from some of the events in my early life came from a lack of explanation. It is vital to take the time to communicate well when interacting with children. Children sense everything, more so than adults, who tend to get caught up in their own reality, so much that they themselves become unaware. Children spend all their time absorbing their environment as though they are sponges absorbing all the information, both spoken and unspoken, that surrounds them.

In dance teaching or anything else, it helps to explain why things are done a certain way. No one likes being told to blindly follow the rules, and children are certainly no exception, and there is no reason not to explain. There is such a rich tradition behind classical ballet training. From explaining the origin of a step or the reasons behind certain studio etiquettes, it's crucial to find ways to incorporate these practical lessons so that the students understand where these traditions came from.

I start teaching children when they are about three years of age, sometimes younger. In my ballet 1 class, my students are around five years of age, and they respond best when things are explained in full detail; anyone who has had a four- or five-year-old in the house knows of the never-ending series of questions. Although sometimes it's hard to satisfy all those young minds in a class, I still stand firmly that giving them more information is the best way to maintain their full attention. Find creative ways to describe the origin of a step, either as a story, a sound, or a rhyme. It enriches the lesson and the practice, and when students are given explanations that they relate to, they are inclined to show their family and friends which, in return, triggers enthusiasm, which we will discuss later in another rule.

Clear explanation is key to fully connect with the child's mind. A simple explanation as to why the arm should be in a certain position will make the difference between them just doing it and them remembering it forever. Take the time to talk with them about the creation of ballet, performing in a large theater, and needing to create each line so it is never-ending when seen on a large stage. There is absolutely nothing random about ballet at this point. Explain, explain, explain, and continue to educate yourself so you never run out of answers.

Most of my students, especially in ballet 1 through 3, know their exercises by heart. It is not unusual in those classes for one of my younger students to raise his/her hand and tell me that I skipped an exercise or did not use the right music for it. In a nutshell, my younger ballet students give me no slack whatsoever. Kids are smart. They may not be fully grown yet, but their awareness is there.

I remember a specific memory, and it must have been within a few months of me teaching children on the Cape. I showed up one day wearing a new lipstick color. It wasn't a bright red, and it wasn't obvious, but there was not one child who did not notice it as they arrived for their lesson. I wasn't surprised so much that they noticed this small change, as children are very aware of their surroundings, but it confirmed my intuition. There is no tricking them, and they know what you are trying to do. They know whether you are comfortable or not doing what you're doing, and fundamentally, they just want to be told what is going on.

Over the last ten years, my students have helped me build and develop a lot of my classes. Some of the material that I started with was tailored as I kept noticing what children respond best to. My philosophy has pretty much always been that listening to students really helps improve and shape the instruction that we want to give them.

I used to think that listening too much to students would make me look like I didn't know enough myself, but I have been teaching for long enough to not second-guess myself in that way. It is my belief that the only shame is to not listen to children, as they can make a crucial contribution to the way teachers should teach.

So try it. You know those days when you can't seem to rally the class, and the energy is high? I respond by just sitting everybody down and talking about why we are here. I never get angry or lose control; it's not to say that I haven't in the past, but for my sanity and theirs, I find that sitting everyone down and getting on the same page, whether they are four years old or 17, is the best way. You'll be surprised at how the dynamic changes. Level up with children. Tell them more. Empower them with knowledge so they feel connected to the moment.

student in class

Chapter 2: La Mise En Scène [Setting the Scene]

Growing Up and Away

My dad and his soon-to-be girlfriend met a few months after my mom left. The new woman rented the upstairs level of the house we were living in and moved in with her two children: a girl one year older than me, and a boy a year younger than my brother. It was great at first; she was great. She was assertive, outspoken, and resourceful. She knew how to get what she wanted—and she wanted my dad.

Living with my brother, my dad, my dad's new girlfriend, and her two children seemed like the best thing that could have ever happened to all of us. She seemed to fill the role of the mother we felt we no longer had, and we truly loved her. I was young still, probably eight by then, and I was eager for this new woman to fill the role of the mother in my life. I even started to believe she and I looked alike. I viewed her as the mother I was always meant to have. She started making things for me that she would make for her daughter: clothes, hair pieces, jewelry, and such. We were taking bubble baths with her kids, we were using conditioner for our hair, cream for our face, and we were eating fresh vegetables. We quickly found that having a woman in the house dramatically improved the quality of our lives.

Those first months while they were there were some of the happiest in my life, and there was so much joy in the air. All the kids got along; we would play together, fight one another, and be merry. I wish the story could end there.

As in any reconstructed family, a certain amount of adjustment needs to take place, no matter how well-intentioned everyone is. When you blend two families, there are going to be differences in how they do things: what they eat, how they dress, spend money, do homework, or celebrate birthdays—it is a great learning platform. But there was no formal structure to our blended family life. It was never my dad's strength to create a structure, at least not at home. He didn't like conflicts, so he dealt with it by withdrawing. He would just close his eyes and pretend everything would disappear.

On the other hand, anyone who knew his new girlfriend would probably consider withdrawal a wise way to resolve an argument with her. She was an explosive redhead who, when mad, would make anyone shy away from any firm opinion they might hold. I remember a time when she left my dad, my brother and I on a camping ground overnight with no car simply because they had a fight. I think it was something about my dad thinking he should take a few days away with just the two of us, his two children. We had all the food in our tent. By the next morning, the raccoons had moved in and none of us got much sleep. I don't think doing things any other way than how she wanted it was ever an option for my dad, and this became apparent quickly. He seemed to be under her spell. Although now I can appreciate having seen the love that they had for each other, I also feel they could have kept a little more of it for the bedroom. I remember early on in the new setup with her in the house, I was woken up by what I thought was someone being sawed in half in my father's room. I remember trying to explain at breakfast the next day that I had trouble sleeping because I kept hearing the sound of a saw going back and forth and the sound of someone screaming. I never got much explanation on that one, but it stopped shortly after. In any case, everything was really fine until the shit started hitting the fan.

After a few months of living together, my new stepsister started to dislike sharing her mother with me. She told her mom, "You like her more than me," and that was it; it was all over. That talk changed everything. My dad's girlfriend closed up completely to me and my brother. She started ignoring us, pushing us aside. Soon enough, even just living there was going to be too much.

Maybe my dad was more concerned about work and providing enough to feed everyone in the house, but he didn't seem to realize we no longer had the opportunity to speak at the kitchen table. It seemed to always be all about his girlfriend's children. I thought that maybe it is more a mother's job to support the children in their daily accomplishments. My dad's girlfriend was a great mom; great moms make sure their children are heard, appreciated, loved, respected, well-dressed, and undefeated. She just didn't want to have to be a great mom to my brother and me.

My brother once spent half the day in the bathroom being punished for something silly he had done on his ninth birthday. I know we were both a bit wound up at times, but that was just mean.

By the time I turned twelve, we moved into another house with new rules. It was basically forbidden for my brother and me to attract any attention to ourselves. One of the attention-seeking behaviors that had to be remedied was playing the piano. I had studied piano for four years, so I suppose my stepmom saw my practicing as wanting to show off or brag about making music. It's not that I was really any good, but it still just seemed like a weird rule. Perhaps it reminded her of my mother or perhaps it was the noise, but whatever the reason, there was nothing I could do. The bottom line was: no piano.

By that age, I was also dancing quite a bit. I was taking all sorts of classes after school, and I loved it. I was discouraged from dancing around the house, and I don't know if it was just a way to keep the competition down or if there was really something offensive about my success or talent. I did take it personally, however, that my ballet recitals were a taboo subject in the house and that any dance moves I performed were seen as a public offense. Not once did the family come see me dance, not even when I danced with the professional ballet company in Montreal.

I never struggled with doing homework, and I genuinely enjoyed learning and studying. The fact that school came easy for me made the subject of grades another taboo subject at the dinner table; to bring up my academics was to be perceived as vain. These matters may sound trivial, but I felt rejected and disregarded. I felt that my family didn't care about me. It seemed, at least, that they wanted to hear as little about me, my interests, and my successes as humanly possible.

The same was true during our vacationing. Every summer, we used to vacation on the shores of Cape Cod; without fail, I'd get an ear infection every summer as soon as we started swimming. My stepmom used to tell me and everyone else in the family that it was something I was doing just to attract attention. She didn't want to hear about it and didn't want anyone else to pay any attention to it. To her, I was ruining everyone's vacation on purpose in vain.

From my own experience with children, I would say that an ear infection is not a first pick when it comes to faking an illness. I can see how since nothing was working to bring me any kind of recognition in the family, faking an illness would have been a good way to garner some kind of loving attention. Truthfully, however, my inclination at the time was really simply trying to disappear.

I never faked my ear infections. I learned so for sure a few years ago at age 30 while I was vacationing with my mom in the tropics. She pulled out her cosmetic bag as we were getting ready to go to the beach and said:

"I brought drops and cotton balls for you. You have swimmer's ear, don't you?"

I looked at her and asked, "What?"

"You have swimmer's ear. You had drains put in your ears when you were a child. If you go underwater, you have to put drops and cotton in them."

So, that day I found out that I have "swimmer's ear," which means that I pretty much get an automatic ear infection if I put my ears underwater. Where was this information all those years ago when we summered on Cape Cod? There I was, on a beach with my mom at thirty years old, and suddenly she was back, ready to play mom again. I could hardly believe my ears. I was suddenly overcome with both anger and self-pity because she never told me. Someone could have helped me take care of my ears. I never had that kind of care, not until that moment. I told myself that I am an adult now, and I don't want my mom bringing me drops. She can keep her drops. Everyone can keep their drops.

During the few years of living at my dad's, my feelings of rejection only intensified. Feeling unimportant and unloved, I started to surround myself with other kids who also felt like life was unfair: girls on drugs, pickpockets, you name it. Luckily, I enjoyed my friends' company more than I enjoyed taking part in their specific lifestyles. Still, I was tipping in the wrong direction.

Growing up in my dad's house, I spent a few years watching my stepmom and her two children have breakfast together in the dining room. My dad and brother didn't have to wake up as early to get ready for the day, as my dad worked later and would drop off my brother who went to another school. I would prepare my breakfast in the kitchen alongside my stepmother and her two kids. She was set on not includ-ing me in their breakfast ritual, which she considered their private time. As a result, I ate breakfast by myself in the kitchen, witnessing through the doorway what having a mom could look like.

My dad's girlfriend chose not to include me as part of her family, and there was not much I could do about it. No amount of screaming and fussing would have helped; her decision was made. I guess the hard part was realizing that when it came to my dad, he did not consider her children less than his. If anything, it was the other way around. And now, my stepbrother lives in my dad's apartment in downtown Mon-treal. Both he and my stepsister have worked extensively alongside my dad over the last ten years. He's been more than supportive to both his girlfriend's (now wife) children financially and otherwise. It is still hard to
understand what my brother and I did wrong to not deserve the same privileges, both then and still now.

me & my brother

Retreating in the United States

At 14, my life suddenly got worse. I was in the habit of not always coming back home at night. My goal was to try to spend as little time at home as I could, and I decided I would not let them know where I was. I didn't think they cared at all about me, so I tested the limits. It didn't go well. I guess they were looking for me one night, and I hid at one of my friend's house. I don't recommend anyone experimenting with testing the limits because it really doesn't work well. A few days later, my dad's girlfriend told my dad: "It is going to be your daughter or me." Take a wild guess as to who moved out that same night? He asked me to pack up a few things and dumped me at my mom's. I took my toothbrush and whatever else a 14-year-old needs to survive.

My dad drove me to my mother's tiny little apartment, where I would have to sleep on the couch. She didn't want me there, and she was clear about it. I was crowding her space, but here I was. There was no closet and no bed. 14 Who needs privacy? I had a nice little corner of the living room floor to put my pile of stuff. My mom's whole apartment had to be no more than four hundred square feet. She used to clean her clothes by hand and bathe in a tiny bath in a filthy looking bathroom. My dad and girlfriend were not kidding around. After this, I thought life was a freaking joke.

There was about a month left of school. School was walking distance from my dad's house, but while living with my mother, I had to take about 45 minutes of public transportation to get to school on time. I had no idea what I was going to do once school was out for the year. I couldn't stay at my mom's; she could hardly take care of herself, so she surely couldn't take care of me. In fact, she flat out told me that she didn't want to have me there. I felt homeless. I was homeless.

It took me a while to figure out my next step. It took a while to believe there was going to be a next step.

No one was surprised when my mom hit rock bottom after the death of my brother. I think she may have had issues prior to his death, but grief had now given her a whole insanity ticket. Music didn't cure her like we thought it might. If anything helped, it was her newfound love of yoga and meditation. It might have been slightly off from the mainstream, but at least she was out of the house and not stuck to the keys of her piano. The yoga practices seemed to be a less harmful way for her to attempt self-improvement. It seemed less isolating and compulsive. If nothing else, she was reaching out to others, and to me, anything that helped her do that was welcome.

A couple years after she left the house, I was nine, and my brother and I started being dragged to chants and other types of gatherings in a meditation center in town. At this point, we were visiting her every other weekend. Soon enough, we were driving more than six hours each way to visit an ashram in upstate New York. The ashram was housed in three large buildings the size of very large hotels. Like a hotel, each building had rooms to stay in as well as lobbies, gardens, fountains, etc. This retreat center was a beautiful place to be—it was luxurious living combined with the sacred energy one feels walking into a place of worship.

Transportation between the three main buildings was provided so that even young children could get around. From the time I was nine years old, we spent most of our vacation time with our mom in the retreat center. It soon became her favorite place to go for weekend getaways, vacations, and holidays. Of course, there were advantages for her bringing us there. For one, she didn't really have to take care of us. Meals were organized so she didn't have to try to cook for us. She didn't need to entertain us or bond with us. She would simply check in, get us settled in the room, and be off and running to the best of what the ashram had to offer.

I think it is fair to say that we didn't see much of our mother during these ashram visits. She was hard to find, and when we did finally locate her, she would be completely out of it, as if she were intoxicated by all the chanting and meditation practices. We were on one of those visits during our Christmas vacation one year; she signed up for a weeklong intensive course, leaving us to entertain ourselves once again. She told us a few days before our departure that she decided not to come back home with us.

My brother and I freaked out. Imagine the scene: two young kids, ages 11 and nine, trying to place a collect call home from one of those tiny little phone booths with the accordion doors. My brother was crying, and I didn't know what to think. I didn't know how we were going to get back to Canada from this place. I can only imagine my dad's reaction when he got our call from the United States announcing that our mother was not returning from her "vacation" with us.

We ended up traveling back home with "friends." I remember sitting beside my mother when she met with some of the ashram employees to discuss the arrangement for her extended stay before we returned home. I was right there next to her, and she would say things that made me feel like she had totally forgotten that she had kids. What are you doing? I was inwardly asking her. Don't you have responsibilities?

My mom lived a little over a year at the ashram. I don't know that I ever judged her for it since I was pretty aware that she was just trying to stay alive. Once, though, I learned that my mom was back in town; she had to be in Canada to renew her visa, so she came back, and it just so
happened to be on my twelfth birthday. But she never called. She never told me she was in town. It was my dad's girlfriend who told me. "Your mom's in town, and she didn't even have the heart to come and see you on your birthday." I wish no one had ever told me. I was trying not to take things personally, but that was a hard one to swallow. Especially coming from my dad's girlfriend. I felt beaten down

Needless to say, when I ended up on my mom's couch at age 14, she and I had to start from scratch. Being rejected is hard, and once it happens, you almost expect it. You expect people to do wrong by you, to let you down, to leave you behind, and to forget about you. So you almost create it or seek it out as the normalcy. As a young teenager, I started setting myself up for rejection unconsciously. I got used to being misunderstood and felt that everyone had given up on me. I believed that I didn't deserve to be cared for; feeling fundamentally alone was easier to bear than feeling rejected again. And then events happened so a little bit of hope could come back.

Finding My Inner Temple

I stayed on my mother's couch for a few weeks, just long enough to finish the school year. Then I called the ashram and asked if they would let me visit for the summer; I was still only 14. I'm not sure whether or not the people at the ashram knew the circumstances of my being there, but in any case, they took me in and found me a guardian. They assigned me to teach dance to the little kids in the summer camp. The fact that I couldn't really speak English didn't seem to be an obstacle. I could say a few words here and there but not in sentences. I think the only thing I managed to say to the little kids in my first class after I introduced myself was "follow me." I was struggling to express myself to say the least but I was welcomed with open arms. I can't say that I was happy or sad to be there at the time; part of me already gave up on people. I just couldn't believe people were trying so hard to make space for me when nobody at home seemed to give a crap, wherever that was.

If that summer at the ashram hadn't happened, I probably wouldn't be around today to tell the tale. During those summer months, not only did I enhance my English, but I also learned that maybe I could accept being cared for, at least in ways that were not too obvious.

For example, I had a guardian at the ashram, but I didn't want to spend much time with her. I didn't feel I needed anyone to check over me. I didn't tell anyone when I started my period; I was not going to start confiding in a stranger. I stayed in a dorm with a bunch of people, but I still kept to myself. I thought I was supposed to be alone, and staying busy doing things to help out felt good.

That summer softened me up a bit. Sometimes the external space we seek to be comforted in, to be reassured in, turns out to really be an internal experience. In the practice of meditation, I found a space to rest my mind, and I found a space to rest my aching heart. Somehow that new internal experience was giving me a new sense of freedom, and that freedom was letting me believe my external reality could one day change as well.

I learned very old sacred chants. I learned to play sacred music and chants that sped up with the rhythm of the drums. I learned how to do rituals with sacred objects. I learned to offer selfless service as a spiritual practice.

I felt accepted in the ashram. I was assigned responsibilities, and it felt good to do things that people appreciated. It made me feel important, accepted, and appreciated. I still didn't know where I was going at the end of the summer, but at least I didn't feel as alone internally. My heart was filling with love again. Things were going to be fine. This experience of chanting and meditation brought me a strong sense of inner freedom: it opened me up to an awareness of wellness and serenity. It is obvious to me now that the greatest gift I received at 14 was the experience of a sacred space inside myself that no one else could spoil, that no one else could damage, that no one else could take away.

The word "truth" in Sanskrit means "that which does not change." In the Indian scripture, it is said that the true self is the one that does not change. This notion of knowing this part of me that does not change made me less vulnerable to the rest of the world. I learned that there is a part of me that will always be strong, courageous, and unaffected by the circumstances of my life. The part of me that has not changed over all the years is my true self: my enthusiasm, my playfulness, and my dedication. Emotions can change; my state of mind and heart shifts all the time. My awareness of the unflinching self within became the anchor on which I could now rely on during the wildest of life's storms. And that is where the next golden rule took birth.

Juillet, 1991

J'ai le goût d'ecrire de ce coté... parce que je suis dan
en autre monde et dans le monde où je suis, c'est
l'intérieur que l'on travail; l'exterieur sert à don
un sens à nos mouvements et sert d'enveloppe
pour protéges notre coeur, nos poumons, le chagr
toutes les choses qu'on montre moins aux-autres.

July '91
Notes from my visit at the Ashram in the summer
1991

"I feel like writing on this side of the page.. because
in the world where I am now, it is the inside that we
focus on. The outside world serves to give a sense to
our movements and serves as an envelope to protect
our hearts, our lungs, our sadness… all the things we
show less to others"

Golden Rule 2
Movement is Born in Stillness

Finding my own inner temple was a catalyst to the way I would live and experience my life both as a dancer and as a dance instructor. It is my experience of meditation and chanting that led me to start feeling the art of dancing more deeply. I would spend sometimes an hour or two in a sitting position doing spiritual practices and be amazed at the intensity of life that would arise within the still body.

As I found comfort in the stillness of my own body, I ironically started to really understand movement. I started to feel within the still body how much life and movement existed. Stillness pulls me back inside myself, and there, in my own inner temple, the joy of dance and movement is what I find. Within the still body lies dance.

Cultivating that stillness is a simple way to teach students to tune in with themselves prior to starting something, dance related or not. Connect with yourself. Breathe. Focus your mind, then let movement be something meaningful, filled with something unique, something that exists now in the present: you.

This idea of stillness in the ballet class isn't new. In ballet class, it is customary for students to stay still before and after exercises. Throughout my own training, I had teachers who would have us hold our fifth position with our arms down in first position or bras bas for quite a while before starting each exercise. What I instill in my classes is a bit more relaxed than that, even though it may look the same from the outside. As a student is asked to hold either their first, third or fifth position before starting an exercise, have them take a moment to breathe, relax, and get centered on what they are about to do.

This concept is pretty integrated in the practice of yoga. In yoga, we hold position, but the breath still flows in and out softly, without \ tension, with just the right amount of energy to keep the form and until it naturally transforms into another pose or comes back to standing still.

Learning to hold our body still and ready before letting the dance begin centers us back within ourselves. It all starts with the mind, being in the now, getting the attention back in the room, on the task, and stop
completely. Fidgeting is not an option if you are trying to learn to have full control of your body for artistic expression. It always starts in stillness. It starts with a calm, relaxed body, a breathing body, and an attentive mind.

Music can be a partner in learning stillness by encouraging dancers to listen deeply to the music before the movement starts. We performed "Les Sylphides" a few years ago with the older students at the studio, and it was a great platform to focus the teaching on stillness. So much of "Les Sylphides" is about moving from that stillness, similar to a moving painting. When that perfect peacefulness is reached on stage as a group and within each dancer, it is such a delectable, soulful movement where stillness and movement dance hand-and-hand with pure grace and mindfulness.

So yes, dance is a wonderful platform to teach discipline and the beauty of movement, but it's also perfect for teaching the importance of stillness. As much importance we put on teaching students how to move, put the same amount of intention teaching them how to be still. Staying in first position is a hard skill to master when you are five, and it is sunny outside. But in so many ways, the mastery of the art of ballet will come with the mastery of the still body.

In order to perfect many advanced dance steps, a dancer will need to be able to find stillness within each step. For example, for a dancer to turn multiple times in a row like a figure skater, they will have to find stillness in the position to continue turning as much as the

momentum will take them. The same is true when it comes to floating a jump in the air, balancing on pointe, or holding a position after a demanding
variation. Stillness is the key to acquiring control and perfecting many dance moves; it's knowing when to push and when to hold still. Let students familiarize themselves with what stillness is early on. It will not only give them focus in their work, but it will also give them a connection with themselves that provides real comfort to the soul.

Eveline at eighteen

Chapter 3: La Repetition Technique [The Technical Rehearsal]

Going Back to an Empty Room

We all know life is not always as easy as we'd hope, and sometimes when things start turning bad, it may continue as bad for quite some time before it starts getting better. Apparently being thrown out of the house the summer I went to live at the ashram was not enough. It seemed that there was still too much of me that had been left behind in my dad's house. I didn't expect to continue living at my dad's house, but he
technically still had full custody of me. I had no place to bring my belongings to, so I never packed them up, but when I returned to my dad's house after the summer at the ashram, I came back to an empty room.

I thought that maybe they were thinking that with my busy schedule, they would give me a hand and move my things out of the room for me, but that wasn't the case. They put only some of my stuff in a box and gave the rest away. I always figured they were my own things to move. They kicked me out; wasn't that enough already? Couldn't they have given me a little time, just a little time to pack up my things and not feel completely insignificant?

Having your stuff given away while you are gone is disheartening. It makes you feel like you're dead to everyone else. Most of us are not comfortable giving away people's stuff, even when they are dead. It wasn't that I was 21 and went to college for three years. I was 14. Today, I teach 14-year-old girls, and I see that for them, there is a lot of meaning in all the little things they own. It's as though girls of that age are preparing to play house with miniature versions of all the stuff they'll one day own for real. I understand that sometimes, for whatever reason, things need to be moved to make room for other things, but that was not the case for me. My dad's house was large enough, and everyone had a bedroom of their own.

When my father's mother passed away, shortly after that, something similar happen. In her will, she gave me all of her sewing materials, including her machines. She was a professional seamstress for most of her life and spent the last year teaching me how to sew on the week-ends. I loved it. Her sewing machines were a great gift for me and a souvenir of our time together. A week after the wake, my dad's girlfriend gave away the sewing machines to her children's school without saying a word to me.

Shocking? No. Sad? Yes. I adored my grandmother. She travelled all the way from Holland to Canada just to marry my grandfather. She spoke Flemish and still wrote to family members back home in Flemish. She had grown up in a well-established family. My grandparents met during World War II, and she left everything to be with him. When she moved to Montreal, she found out that my grandfather was not as well off as he made it sound to her. As a result, she ended up working most of her life just to make ends meet. She was a seamstress, and they formed a company together making curtains.

I'm sure she never shed a tear about her life not turning out the way she expected. Unfortunately, things never got better for her. My grandfather had dementia in the last years of his life and managed to completely alienate both of them from the rest of the neighborhood with his loud and inappropriate comments. When the neighbors began to get upset about her husband's outbursts, she just started leaving the house less and less, making sure she wouldn't cross anyone's path.

It's a shame that she moved into the apartment above my dad's house because she became even more alienated, though this time it wasn't by strangers. I was thirteen then. My dad's girlfriend claimed my grandmother smelled, so she wasn't allowed to have dinner with us.

Instead, she would have all of her meals by herself upstairs. I was too young to do anything about it. It should have been possible to have someone help her take a shower or a bath. How can you love a man and not love his mother? How can you love a man and not love his children?

I was with my grandmother the night she started having pain in her arm. I remember holding her; she was scared, and I wanted her to be safe. I told her I knew she would be okay if she had to die because she was a good woman. She was, and she was the best. I was 14 when she passed away, just a few months after I was moved out.

Better Mom Than Not

When I returned from the ashram, my mom moved into a bigger apartment so that I would be able to come live with her. I even got a room to myself. Supposedly, the ashram called my mom and told her she had to take care of me. Mommy Class 101: Take Care of Your Kids. I guess it didn't occur to her that it would be a nice gesture. But she did, at that point, allow me back in. She was able to return to work and regain her footing slowly.

The two of us and the grand piano moved several times after that. It wasn't a small task since every single apartment we moved into was on the third floor or higher. Each move required a crane to lift the piano into our new unit, usually through a window overlooking a busy street.

Living with my mom all over again was no walk in the park either; we fought a lot, and she was oblivious to so many things when it came to me. She had practically given up on raising her kids, so she seemed to think that whatever she was doing now was scoring her bonus points. I remember one fight in particular when I was a senior in high school; I needed a dress for the graduation ball. Everyone else was getting a brand new dress; some of my friends' mothers were even sewing a special dress just to give them exactly what they wanted. Well, not my mother. She refused to spend the money on one. She said to me: "Take a look at my old wedding gown. I think it is back in style. You can wear that."

My mom's wedding dress wasn't that bad, actually; it was soft pink lace, so at least it wasn't as obvious that it was worn before as a wedding gown by my mother. But the issue was the ribbon. It was not enough that I felt I was the only one in the whole school whose mother refused to invest money for their daughter to feel special, or that my body type did no favors for me, as I looked like a stick with no ass or breasts in an empire-style dress. But the only decoration on the dress was an old, more yellow than pink, satin ribbon tied into a bow right in the front of the dress. I suggested to my mom that we change the ribbon on the dress, which turned out to be a bad move. I guess letting me wear the dress was already a major achievement; she responded that the ribbon was fine just the way it was, and I was a spoiled brat. "Maudit enfant gaté," (darned spoiled child) were the words she used—to me, it sounds worse in French. It didn't end there, though: I talked back. I ultimately didn't mind the dress, but I was not going to my prom with that old ribbon on my mom's old dress. I would have preferred to skip the whole event, or more romantically, throw myself off the bridge with the old dress on.

We had a nasty fight that night. She couldn't understand me, and we sparred both verbally and physically. I told her she sucked. I told her she was a bad mother. I told her she was self-centered and greedy. The crazy thing is that my mom actually has a lot of money. When she was sleeping under her piano and practicing 16 hours each day, she lived off the interest of the money she was keeping at the bank in a regular savings account. Realistically, she had the means to buy me a dress; she had the money. But to her, money is best kept in the bank.

It took me several years after I left the country to convince her to purchase a home and stop helping someone else pay their mortgage by paying rent. She listened and paid cash for her home. She ended up tripling her investment in real estate a few years later. Sadly, my mom lives as though something terrible is always about to happen. I can respect that. Terrible things did happen. At least she found what she needed to do in order to live "normally." There probably could have been worse scenarios.

In the end, she agreed to change the ribbon on the dress. It cost us $12 for the new ribbon and I sewed it on myself. It was one ugly fight. It did, however, open the dialogue and establish some ground rules between us. I made sure I never asked my mom for anything again, and she never again referred to me as a spoiled brat.

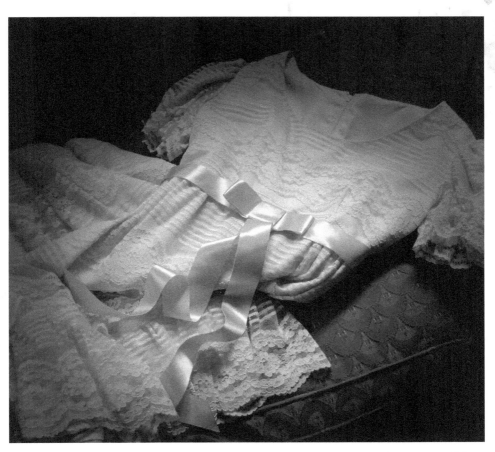

dress with new ribbon

Starting Ballet School

By the time I moved in with my mother, I started ballet school, which I like to think of as the equivalent of military school. It's regimented, and it affects all areas of our life. It's not just something you do; it's something you are or eventually become. I never really considered myself a ballet dancer at the time, but I ached to dance more, and going to a dance-focused high school was a more integrated way to combine schooling and training. The program allowed students to dance every day of the week during regular school hours, and the program was free. Unlike other national ballet schools in the country, this was a public program.

There was a strict auditioning process: not only did they watch us dance, but they had us medically evaluated and carefully measured to make sure we had what they considered a properly proportioned dancer's body. There were 15 dancers in our grade selected from different areas of the province to be a part of this pre-professional high school dance program.

The program was associated with the regular regional high school as well as a music program that was set up similarly to the dance program. In other words, we didn't have to hang out with ballerinas all the time. We did tend to stick together regardless. We didn't exactly fit in or blend in with the other kids. We were usually running around the school, trying to finish putting our hair up into buns or going to class in dance cover-ups so we could quickly get ready for our ballet class later on. There was also the stretching; if you ever lived with a dancer, are a dancer, or know a dancer, then you already know: dancers stretch all the time.

Dancers stretch prior to a class, after a class, and pretty much any-time in between. With a leg on a desk, or stretched back on the floor, or across the neighbor's chair, or during lunch break, we were always stretching. We would usually opt for the floor so we could spread out.

We were training two to three hours every day, five days a week. For the most part, it kept me out of trouble. It's not that I was a trouble-maker, but I had a creative mind, and I was, as far I as I could tell, pretty much parentless. I had a lot of freedom, and I had a lot of ideas on how to use that freedom.

dancer stretching

The academic side of high school was not quite as challenging as the dance element. Prior to changing schools and going into the ballet program, I had been in an advanced program in the first two years of high school in Canada (seventh & eighth grade in the US) near my dad's house. Once I entered the ballet program, the academic classes were less advanced and not as stimulating as a result. My grades were high, so I got a bit of slack. I did better at reading the material than listening, and since all the information was in the books, soon enough my teachers realized they were better off letting me skip class than keeping me around being bored and kind of obnoxious about it. I was done with the math program by Christmas in my graduating year, so they had me paint a mural on the classroom back wall to keep me busy.

Overall it was a great experience, and I was surprised to fall so deeply in love with classical ballet. I joined the program thinking that I would specialize in modern dance in my final year, which was one of the two options. The other option was to stay in classical ballet. I still didn't really identify myself as a ballet dancer, but ballet was kicking my ass, and I liked it that way. I quickly became very serious in my training; I probably pushed my body a bit too hard at times, and like most dancers, I struggled with injuries. My injuries included tendonitis in my Achilles tendon, my hips, and knees. I realize today that the training we received did not focus enough on proper alignment, which may have contributed to my injuries.

The ballet training I received in high school may have been questionable at times. I feel, although it was a reputable school, some of the teaching methods utilized by our teachers were a bit out of line. For example, for most of our high school years, our ballet teacher's nickname for us was "fat marshmallows." Trust me, I love marshmallows just as much as the next person, but it is easy to understand that a marshmallow is not the look you are going for when you are attempting to become a ballerina. We may have been sluggish every now and again, but "fat" is pretty much a word to avoid when teaching young girls.

She would bring in the scale every Friday morning, which is also not the best pedagogical technique to use when dealing with young teenage girls. I understood her intentions, but it might have been a better strategy to include nutrition classes to help us make better food choices so we could keep our bodies lean but strong.

Enticing women not to eat in the middle of their teenage years, which was the subtext of her comments and actions, is not only stupid but dangerous. Of course, I thought I was being clever by denouncing her teaching methods to the school's directors, which she obviously didn't like. She found a way to suspend me from her class for a month. She always found a reason to throw me out within the first 15 minutes of the class every day for four consecutive weeks. She would say my arm was wrong, my timing was off, or she didn't like the way I was doing something at the barre. Granted, I was pretty much a punk and didn't listen very well. I knew she was upset that I was going against her will. Eventually, I understood that keeping my mouth shut was a much smarter approach and would considerably increase my chances of becoming a dancer, especially since I was barely allowed in the class at that point. I wanted to dance, so I had to reform. I was a punk, and punks made bad ballerinas. I reformed, or at least I stopped, all direct rebellious activities.

We never saw a scale after that. I secretly believe that I may have saved some of my classmates some therapy sessions later, so I consider the incident worth it.

My last year of high school also marked the school's 15th anniversary, and the foundation decided to produce a celebratory performance rather than a typical end-of-year concert. It was a beautiful performance in a very large theater downtown, and I was chosen to perform as the soloist for the anniversary gala. This was a great opportunity for me, but it was odd not to have a real end-of-year concert for our last year. It certainly didn't seem fair for some of my classmates who had invested just as much time and energy in the program to not be properly showcased in their last year at the school.

I decided with the class that we, the students, should produce our own concert. We ended up creating a show that allowed each dancer to present something of her own choice on stage, either alone or as a group piece. One student had all of us sing a medley of songs that she arranged; many of us presented dances that we choreographed on our own. Everyone participated in her own way, from creating programs and ordering food for the reception afterwards to designing the show's content and coordinating music and tech.

We were able to raise funds by creating and selling t-shirts to cover the cost of renting the auditorium and everything we needed to put on our own show. The show was a huge success and a real eye-opener for all of us and our ability to really make things happen. We successfully put together a nice program that showed our creativity and talent, and audiences responded by packing the place. With proper alignment and focus, we were able to do great things, and I felt proud of myself for being able to see it all through. I started to build on that new self-realization, and it made me feel eager to continue to do good things that brought people together in a positive way.

I am very grateful for the dance education I received in Canada. It was a great opportunity for me to receive a professional-level training that was both accessible and affordable. But to this day, I am still concerned about the lack of supervision of the ballet masters' teaching techniques by the school. There was never enough scrutinizing of what was really taking place in the classroom. It is tempting to think that ballerinas themselves should know best when it comes to teaching future dancers, but they don't. Most of them were broken down physically and emotionally in their own training, and they were repeating the same patterns onto the new generations.

I understand now that my ballet teacher in high school was probably treating us the same way she had been treated in her earlier years of training -- she just didn't know any better. Trust me, I do believe in compassion, and I can sympathize with what she went through, but I know half a dozen girls who graduated in the years both before and after our class who needed serious therapy after high school because of this woman's abusive teaching techniques. Even now, those women may very well be teaching other young women in the same cutting, self-hating manner in which we were taught. She made it okay to be mean, and it should never be okay. We can't have educators out there making these old mistakes. It is scary to think that to this day, there are still no ways to judge or calculate someone's competence as a dance instructor.

I have seen eating disorders firsthand, and it's not a laughing matter. Teenage women are a delicate breed; they put themselves down enough as it is, dancer or not, but those who have selected the form of dance are especially prone to low self-love simply due to the demands they put on their bodies on a daily basis. There is no need to further cultivate and enhance this low self-esteem among these young women.

There are indeed other ways to teach students the demands of the art form without attacking them as individuals. Cultivating enthusiasm and discipline as a way of showing commitment is not only a much more positive approach to dance education, but it simply works better. Moreover, enthusiasm and discipline are traits that dance students can always apply to other areas of their lives; it is simply teaching them real life skills and resources.

In my

words

Golden Rule 3
Keep the Enthusiasm Alive

Day after day and year after year, I have seen with virtually all of my students that enthusiasm is essential to progress. It is the student's enthusiasm that will drive him/her to success; in turn, no student who has lost enthusiasm will progress.

As instructors, we have to be mindful of our interactions with each student. Corrections to form should serve to find new ways to improve without extinguishing the student's enthusiasm or love for him/herself or the art form. It is the fire behind the work, and it is our energy behind all the hours of training. We need to keep it alive and strong.

Inspire dancers by motivating them to work harder. Remind them of their progress, and remind them of their goals. Work with them, not against them. This idea of breaking down the individual must be revised. Yes, discipline is needed, and yes, controlling the classroom is important for an educator, but it should be done with love and respect for all individuals present in the classroom.

I was a hard student to teach, and I realize that. I didn't let many people teach me many things in my life as a result, but I know the people that did succeed in teaching me did so because they respected me and recognized my passion. I don't want to be judged or put down. If someone can see the love that I have for the things that I do, and if they tell me, "look, do it this way, it will work better," then yes, I want to hear everything they have to say because I want to succeed. We all do.

Putting down students serves absolutely no purpose. Life is hard enough, and there is no need to use dance instruction to make our students more miserable. Learning to work is a blessing, but we are building individuals who have a heart and a mind of their own; we have to be gentle. I know it can be hard at times to teach. Sometimes we all get out of sorts, but we need to remember that enthusiasm fuels our entire life. Feeling that enthusiasm will fundamentally make us feel better about ourselves as an educator, and in the same way, kindling that enthusiasm in our students will also help them feel better about themselves and help them be inspired towards their training.

Enthusiasm brings us back to our own life-force energy. It is our heart. It is our love. It defines us. Keep your students' enthusiasm alive. Let them connect with their love for the art form or activities. Let them be good at it, talk about it, and experience it. And sometimes, remembering how excited we got about something just this once is a feeling that will stay with us forever.

The Story of Rebecca

Several years ago, I had a pretty difficult student in my ballet 1 class. She was constantly seeking negative attention, and she was hard to re-direct. I knew she loved to dance, and she really seem distressed when I would reprimand her misbehaving in class, but she just didn't seem to find a way to follow the group. I'm sure that she was used to getting attention from her negative behavior, so she grew to crave that attention.

After almost six months of trying to redirect her so she would work with the group instead of constantly against it, I came to a point where I decided that I could no longer keep her in the class. Her behavior was too distracting for the rest of the students, and I just didn't want to give any more attention to her misbehaving. So one day after talking to her caretaker, I took her aside and said, "I'm sorry Rebecca, but I don't believe I can teach you dance anymore. You don't listen to me. I can teach you to be a good dancer, but you have to listen to me, and now you don't listen to me, so I can't teach you."

Rebecca was five. Her father was in jail. I believe her mother was working a lot because I barely saw her at the studio. I didn't know much more about Rebecca except that she loved to dance. When I told her I couldn't teach her anymore, Rebecca started to cry. I started to cry shortly after as well because prior to Rebecca, I never told a student that I couldn't teach them anymore. She went home.

The following week, Rebecca came back with her grandmother and asked me very politely if I would give her another chance. I said yes. Rebecca, after that day, became my lead student. She was absolutely impeccable. I complimented her a lot on her good attention and execu-tion, and I'd like to believe that she enjoyed the positive attention for a change. Her grandmother came back the next week and told me Re-becca received a star from school that same week for her good conduct, which had never happened and never thought possible.

Rebecca struggled in school as much as she struggled with following at dance, but I believe that something changed in her then. I could see it: she started believing in herself, and it made a big difference. Rebecca and I became very close. I taught her for four more years after that. She would often come early and tell me about her day. She showed me her report cards and shared other praises she received from school for her good effort. I felt so happy to see her shine in this way.

I remember she came in one day and told me how they were fundraising money so her school could stay open, and it made a big impression on her. She started collecting her quarters to save her school, and I thought it was so sweet. She showed up one day with all her quarters in a bag and informed me she was going to the bank to change them all for dollars. I said, "Listen, Rebecca. How much do you have?" She said, "$12." I said, "Give me your quarters, and I will give you $24." I matched what she gathered, and she looked at me like life was a fairytale too good to be true.

We had a little incident at the end of the school year when Rebecca came to my office crying before class one afternoon. She told me she was very upset because she didn't do well on her test that day in school. She continued crying as she told me the story and said she needed help at home to do her homework and to study. Rebecca said her mother works at night so she's not home with her, and her mom's boyfriend watches TV all night. Once, he sent her to her room with a bag of chips for dinner. She had a TV in her room, and he told her that she was supposed to watch it, and sometimes it stayed on all night. She was hungry the night before and needed more help, and that's why she didn't do well on her test today. I really try not to get involved in my students' lives more than I should. I care a lot as it is, so it's difficult when they tell me personal things about their home lives. I slept on it, not wanting to speak to anyone before really thinking it through, but I was sad for her. I felt it had been a bit of a miracle to get her committed to being the best that she could be and to keep her enthusiasm alive even when she misbehaved. I had so much pride to see how much she aspired to be good at what she did. I tried very gently to tell her mother a few days after that her daughter came to me, pleading that she needed more help with her school work. It didn't seem like a really good topic, so I didn't push it. I didn't bring up the bag of chips or the TV in her bedroom because it still seemed out of place on my part. When I checked in with Rebecca the following week, she was happy again. I think she did get more help at home, but the following month, they stopped coming to the dance center altogether. And I never heard back even though I tried to reach out to them multiple times.

I believe Rebecca's enthusiasm towards dance helped her find her way. I do believe strongly that guiding students in a subject they love, like dance, can help shape their behavior. Of course, it's not everything, but it does provide a great platform for change.

My students are not my kids, and I can't control everything, but I hope that the enthusiasm she felt will stay with her forever. I hope it helps her make the best choices for herself so she can blossom to be the best person she can be.

Chapter 4: La Répétition Musicale [The Musical Rehearsal]

Dancing Through College

When it came time to move on to college, I auditioned to join the professional ballet training program offered as a bachelor's degree with Les Grands Ballets Canadiens in Montreal. The program's affiliation with the world-renowned ballet company made it the best option of having work performing during and after the training.

Even though I started dancing at a young age, a lot of the dancers auditioning for the program had been enrolled in that specific school from the sixth grade. A good friend of mine from elementary school had been in the program since the sixth grade and was auditioning just like me to stay in the program at the college level. In Canada, college starts a year earlier that the US, so we have one less year of high school. While some dancers auditioning had been in the program since age eleven, I was trying to join the program at sixteen.

The school attracted dancers from all over the province, other areas of Canada, and even dancers from the United States and worldwide. One of the girls I became very close friends with traveled all the way from Japan to be a part of this elite program. I was accepted for the six-week summer intensive program, which was the first step in getting into the intensive college program. All of us were to have our interview with the artistic director at some point to hear whether or not we made it into the program.

On the last day of the summer program, I had my interview with the artistic director of the school, and I was the last one to hear back. Of the 60 girls who were accepted into the summer intensive, only 15 would be selected for the fall. The director told me that I wasn't that great, but since I at least was good in school, I'd be able to spend most of my time focused on my dancing, which apparently needed the most attention. It wasn't a great evaluation, but I could live with it. I was in, chosen as one of the 15. By the time we graduated, however, there would be only eight of us left. A few more quit, and one found a job touring before the last year of training.

I went from dancing 10 to 12 hours a week to 18 to 25, and on most weekend nights, I could be found on clubs' dance floors. I would dance and dance then dance some more. I wanted it all: not just the training towards idealized perfection, but also the freedom to keep that wild creative energy that the ballet teachers were so desperately trying to rub out of us. I felt I needed to go dance my heart out to make up for all the hours I spent being forced into a tiny little ballet mold. I had to keep my soul alive.

The training was intense; "brutal" is probably more accurate. To keep up at the professional level of training, we had to show up for ballet class 30 to 40 minutes early just to warm up so we could deliver from the first exercise at the barre what was expected from us. Perfect concentration was demanded. We were instructed to look the same in our pink tights and nylon leotards in the color corresponding to our age level. By the end of the ballet barre, which usually lasted 40 minutes, we were drenched in sweat. And it was just the beginning of the class that would usually last an hour and a half, followed by another hour or two of pointes work, partnering, variations, or other styles of dance before moving to our other dance-related subjects, such as anatomy, music history, dance history, theater, voice, stage makeup, stage design, and choreography.

It is not generally known how highly demanding dance really is. Meeting the demands of the physicality of dance is equivalent to the training of many high-performing athlete such as gymnasts, figure skaters, swimmers, and many others. Ballet is a beautiful art form, but it also requires the dancer to fight the natural inclination to avoid pain every step of the way. Dancing can be physically painful, as it constantly pushes the limits of the body further, so we go to the limit of pain every day. This challenge is addictive in a way. It's extremely satisfying to learn to have so much control over one's body, but it is also a lifestyle where one can never really just walk away from the instrument. We live in our instrument, and the training often makes it hard to see where the end of the road is. There are always ways to make a step better or harder. The limit of dance is pushed constantly, so it's easy to feel that there is no end in sight.

Luckily, dance is also an art, so being genuine, heartfelt, and vulnerable also counts. It's a balance that dancers, probably just like other athletes and artists, have learned to find on their own so that it stays a healthy pursuit.

Cape Cod Dance Centers performance of Gisèle

Learning to Play Piano

Following the path of dance rather than music was not as automatic as it might have seemed. I loved playing the piano as much as I loved to dance, and both go together so beautifully. Growing up, we had a grand piano in my parents' house, and both my mom and dad played. It was an angelic item to me. I just loved the sounds of music.

I was about six years old when I was left home alone for a little while. I prepared a pretty table filled with beverages and food for my parents to come back to. I couldn't find any recorded music to complete the scene the way I had envisioned it, so I sat at the piano, played notes in a way that pleased me, and recorded it. When my parents returned, I played what I had recorded back to them. My mom cried, and she brought the tape to her music teacher who agreed to teach me. She was a very well-known and coveted music teacher at McGill University. I was only six when I started music lessons with her.

In her enthusiasm for what she thought was my giftedness, my teacher perpetually berated me for not holding my hands in the right position while practicing scales up and down the keyboard. I wanted to play the piano because it sounded so beautiful; it had touched my soul somehow, yet now I was being punished for not properly doing an exercise that didn't make any sense to me. It was dry. Some days my teacher gave me stickers because I did well, and some days she didn't. The truth is, once I started taking lessons, I never truly played the piano again in the way that it touched my soul.

Eventually I changed teachers. When my parents separated, I studied with someone else who lived closer to my dad's house. After that, I studied with another woman who was also a McGill associate. She had me take the official ranking test, but I did poorly. By then, there was a lot of stress associated with playing the piano; living at my dad's house was making it practically impossible to play. The only time slot I could find was right after school before anyone else got home. There were also mixed feelings with the instrument because of what my mom was going through and how the piano was practically keeping her away from us. She was spending so many hours playing and so little time with my brother and me that I had trouble losing myself in the experience of music the way I once had.

It was years later when I was finishing high school and entering college that I went back to playing the piano. I lived with my mother then, and I was able to play on the grand piano when she was away. I began playing again for myself and by myself, without a teacher and without guidelines. I just played. I could read music well by this point, so I learned a lot of pieces from music sheets and eventually played them by heart. Once I knew the pieces, I could just focus on the texture, the phrasing, the expressiveness, and I rediscovered what I had loved so much from music. No one could take that away from me.

When we performed "Les Sylphides" as part of our training in college, I discovered how intense my love for music really was. "Les Sylphides" is a beautiful ballet set to a few nocturnes by Chopin. My mom used to play these nocturnes while I was growing up, so I was already very familiar with the music. I think Chopin is one of the best musicians the world has ever known. His music is so gentle, and it cuts right through your heart without any extra notes. It just is what it is: no more and no less, and it pours with emotion.

When I dance to music that touches me, I become like a taut string. I feel I can't be played too hard, as it hurts. I remember being very emotional during the rehearsal process. I would often hold back tears, and it made my heart soar. I wasn't used to being musically touched so much in the classroom. I was surprised to find out one day that my ballet teacher thought I was bored to death during rehearsals for "Les Sylphides." She came up to me and said, "I know this is not your favorite style of dance, but please make an effort."

It was not that I disliked this form of dance, but it was my past with the music. I wanted to scream at my teacher: "My mom is fucked up. She used to play this song to me when I was five."

Of course, I didn't say anything. And even though I wanted to just sit down and play the music for her, I didn't do that either. I never got a chance to tell anyone at the school how I felt about music. When I saw the first scene of "Les Sylphides" unfold, I wished that we could have danced to Chopin just a little slower so as not to disturb the beauty of the nocturnes being played on the piano.

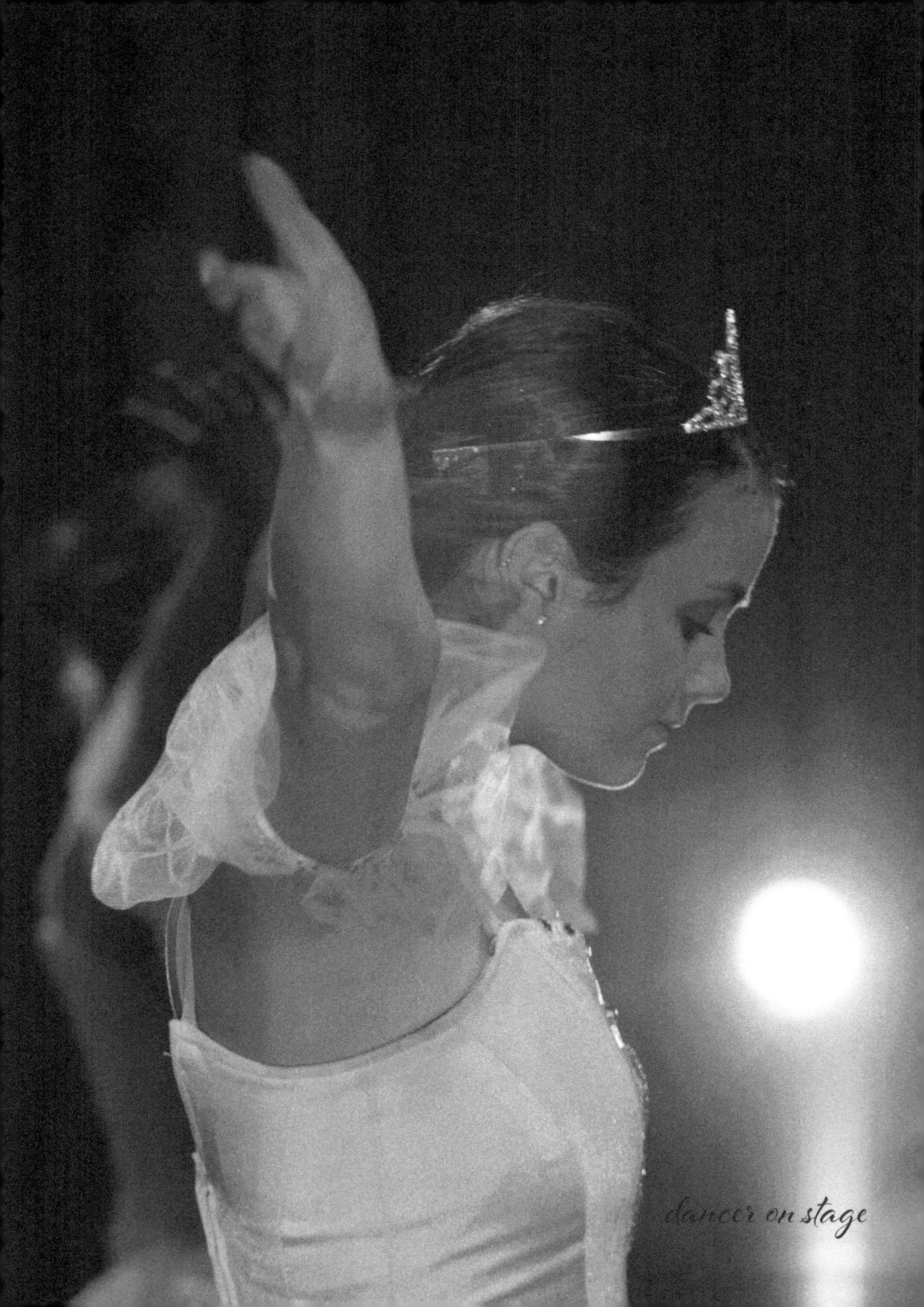
dancer on stage

Golden Rule 4
Let Music Be the Guide

My experiences of music became my ally during my pursuit of dance; my love of music directly supports my love of dance, and they walk and in hand. Many times, it has been my love of music that has gotten me through some rough times while performing or rehearsing. There are many ways in which music nourishes my love for choreography and the dance form.

In my dance teaching, I often let music take the lead when it comes to creating exercises and inspiring the dances. Dance was born from music, and sensitivity to music is essential to dancing well. Implementing dance education with introduction to music is a great way to sensitize the students to the art of music.

For example, we created a summer camp where students are asked to create characters, a story, and a dance to showcase that character. It's a great camp, as it gives students the opportunity to go beyond the dancing and create something that they love. It is very engaging for the students, and it gives us a great platform to teach other elements that make up the dance world, such as costumes, masks, etc., and as part of the process, the students pick music for their creation, which then gives us a moment to introduce them to music history.

I have taught this camp many times now, and each time I sit down with the students to pick their music, I can see the same expression on their faces. They are truly listening, and for some, they are truly listening for the first time. "Is this music really portraying what my character wants to convey in this dance? Does this really have the right feel for my creation?" When it comes to making decisions, we have to be informed, and suddenly things start to connect.

The students feel responsible for their character, and they want their production to be perfect. They want just the right music. Yes, it's a camp, but getting kids to understand the subtlety in music is hard, and I can tell you with absolute certainty, you must let them be in charge of their own creation, and they'll want to dive in. It may not be called formal education, but it is something else: it is call owning, and when you feel that, you want to do well with it.

Sitting down with kids and listening to music for a couple hours is probably just as good as giving them musical training. Those kids are listening hard, and I see them talking to each other. "Is that good? Is that too fast, too slow, too fun, too mysterious, too dark, too upbeat?" That's what music brings: everything. Give them a chance to explore that. I believe this simple exercise teaches them to see the variations in tempo, phrasing, and sometime even the overall emotional content of what a piece of music can carry.

It is my experience that dance students with a solid background in music or a sensitivity to music make better dancers. It is hard to teach someone how to be musically inclined, but a sensitivity to sound and rhythm can be developed over time. A teacher of mine who danced as one of Nureyev's partners told us more than once that the difference between a dancer who is going to be a soloist and a dancer who is going to be a principal dancer is musicality, not flexibility, not strength, not beauty, but musicality.

I have no doubt that this is true. On a separate note, another appealing thing about putting music first is that it puts the attention back on the art form. So often, the training can lead to a false sense of self, either feeling too good or not good enough about ourselves as dancers. Focusing back on music brings our attention back to the art and the reason one chooses to dance in the first place: to express ourselves. Focusing on the music will ensure that dancers focus back on dance as an art form and not their ego.

student onstage with live orchestra

Chapter 5: Le Réchauffement Sur Scène
[Warm-up on Stage]

Struggling Through Injuries

Our training continued without a break during the first two years of the college program. Taking breaks was not advisable at the time, so we went through all six semesters in two years without summer or holiday vacations. Once those six semesters were completed, we were brought upstairs to the company.

At one point in my training, my teacher told me that he would understand if I decided not to come back the next day. I had very severe shin splints in the tibia of both legs, which made me collapse frequently in class. The shin splints progressed all the way up to the femur in both legs, causing me to lose sensation completely and collapse in a miserable combination of numbness and pain. However, I never thought it was a real option not to come back; I instead thought my teacher was testing me, so I didn't want to give up. I had to learn to push even harder, and eventually the injury went away on its own.

I struggled with injuries during most of my training, and I still deal with physical issues from dancing from time to time. It's not realistic to use the body so vigorously and not expect aches and pains in the process. It is tough to deal with injuries, however, and not just physically. Maybe I read too much into things, but I always found it hard not to translate an injury as a sign that I should have been doing something else or something different. With proper technique and the help of a capable physical therapist or alignment specialist, injuries should not reoccur too often, but then again, sometimes it takes getting injured a few times for dancers to really understand the need to make an adjustment in their training techniques or habits.

Injuries have three sources: an accident, overexertion, or misalignment. The first thing one needs to do when dealing with an injury is determine which of the three types it is. It is very important to continue treating the injured area and to also make the correct adjustments in your basic techniques so the injury doesn't reoccur. On the other hand, a long-term injury could also have been caused by an isolated misstep, which may require getting a quick realignment from a chiropractor or osteopath.

Handling an injury caused by overexertion is tough, as an overexertion injury comes with the complication of making a dancer susceptible to further deterioration, arthritis, stress fractures, and other injuries that could last even longer.

Dancers now have the option of reaching out to doctors who are familiar with or even specialize in treating dancers. General sports medicine practices generally don't address the multiple and specific issues of the dancer's body. For example, dancers tend to be extremely flexible, which can create a series of bodily issues that are specific to dancers. Additionally, dancers are used to working through pain. Ballet dancers, especially, are taught to not respond to normal physical warnings from a very young age, particularly through the process of practicing pointe.

Some doctors and therapists in Boston and New York have developed a new field of "dance medicine." Dance medicine practitioners understand that dancers undergoing surgery need to not only regain full mobility but also retain all of their flexibility.

If a dancer is injured and needs help finding a good dance physician or therapist, it is imperative to search for dance medicine resources online. The Children's Hospital in Boston has a great dance medicine department, and other hospitals are now understanding and providing resources specific to dancers. As the field of dance medicine grows, there is no reason not to find the help needed. It could make the difference between dancing and not dancing again.

Golden Rule: 5
Dance Training is a Path, Not a Leap

Over the years I have had several students deal with injuries during their training. It is simply part of it, and often it is there to teach us something. Injuries usually happen for a reason. There is often a weakness that made the dancer prone to the injury that occured, and the healthiest approach is looking at the injury as an opportunity to get stronger than one was before the injury.

It's easy to feel that training has stopped when an injury occurs, and it is hard to deal with when students are so eager to push forward in their training. Being stopped because of a sprained ankle or a knee injury is incredibly disappointing.

As we direct dance students toward becoming the best they can be, remind them that it is a path and never just one leap. Hopefully dancers are training for a long career, so learning to pace ourselves as dancers is key. Students should develop and fine-tune their skills along the path at their own pace. Seeking specific results in an unrealistic time frame can lead to both physical injury and another kind of injury: a feeling of inadequacy. Training a dancer takes time and patience.

A student sprained her ankle in gym class once, the day before dress rehearsal for the Nutcracker performances. She was devastated. It was such a difficult incident, and yet, what can we do? We just have to accept it. Recently, a student's pointe shoe ribbon came untied on stage, and she rolled off of it, spraining it. She was out for a few months. It is heart-wrenching, but on the positive side, these girls were stronger than ever after it.

First, the longing to dance while healing builds up and strengthens a student's love for the art form, and that is very powerful. Second, the post-injury physical therapy can dramatically strengthen a dancer in areas where, without the injury, the weakness may have stayed. Third, the body awareness that comes from dealing with an injury is something that is very hard to teach. We can talk about it, and we can help students slow down enough to feel sensation in the body while doing specific exercises, but really, unless you are forced to stop, most of us just keep on pushing forward.

It is our job as dance teachers to keep our students balanced by offering a curriculum that provides guidance on body alignment, thorough warm-up routines, and strengthening exercises. There are no overnight achievements in dance training; it all gets built up slowly. The keys to successful dance training are repetition, commitment, and doing it all over again tomorrow.

Regular training and personal goal-setting are both key elements in developing a healthy dance journey. For example, to enhance one's overall strength and flexibility, a dancer may want to add regular stretching and strength training a few days a week. Stretching too much too quickly, like striving to achieve a complete split too soon, can hurt a young, growing dancer. Learning how to devote time to the improvement of one's skill is something that should be done in a consistent manner.

The young girl who sprained her ankle on stage because of her pointe shoe ribbon was so distressed because she didn't want to fall behind. It was hard to watch. The students all work so hard, and we are lucky that the group dynamic is good. We do our best to keep the competition between the students under control so that they are eager to do well and move forward. Stopping for a few months is really not what anyone wants to hear, but again, dance training is a path, not a leap. While suffering an ongoing injury, most students will still be able to learn by watching, stretching, and strengthening. They can work to retrain some muscle groups that may have been working less and relax other muscle groups that may have been overworked. This will help reaffirm that dancing is what they want to keep doing, either as a career or a hobby.

Learning to deal with setbacks is huge, and they don't stop as we get older. To learn to make the best of the situation we are dealt with is a lesson that we can carry on forward because life is a path, and every step of it counts.

students backstage

Chapter 6: L'Espacement Sur Scene
[Spacing on Stage]

Choreographing Dance

I started creating dances in my first dance studio when I was about nine years old. During most of my childhood, when dancing was what gave me my own sense of happiness, my love of dance was derived in large part from my love of choreography.

At 12, two friends and I created a piece that we performed in a choreography contest. We made three large masks and contacted an African dancer who showed us some moves that we incorporated into the dance. I remember taking the bus to the opposite side of town to meet this African lady who was glad to introduce us to traditional African dancing. We ended up dancing with her for a whole afternoon in her living room. It was a blast.

At the time, I was enrolled in a local jazz studio program. I auditioned to be in the studio's intensive program, but they didn't think I was advanced enough. I was heartbroken, and since we weren't allowed in all the other more advanced classes, my two friends and I started using studio space to create our own dance. Looking back, the dance we choreographed was quite innovative, especially given our ages. We started with the African theme and continued in juxtaposed solos in jazz, modern, and ballet so we all got to dance in our own style. We received really positive feedback from the audience in response to what we created.

The jazz studio that organized the choreography contest was impressed with our dedication and accepted all three of us into the intensive program the following year.

It was one of these friends who talked me into auditioning for the high school program in dance. She wanted to go, and we ended up attending together. She was always a great ally, and we ended up finishing our high school years in that school together. She continued her training in modern dance, while I stayed with the ballet, and in our final year, we created a piece together. Her class performed barefoot side-by-side with my class dancing on pointes. We found ways to pair each modern dancer with a ballet dancer, and the combination worked really well. It was unusual, especially at the time, and people liked it.

In college, I started retreating to the empty studios after my dance classes to work on my own movement, style, and choreography. This was my way of making sure I kept my own identity. I soon became close friends with a girl who also seemed to have a similar need to keep her expressive self alive. We both had been working on little bits and pieces of material, which we ended up combining into a piece that we called, "Major Freak Out." Probably because we were spending so many hours training in a pretty rigid manner, a lot of our movements looked like we were trying to break free from something. We were both expressing a similar feeling which, side-by-side, created an explosive effect.

This is what led to me to graduating with a scholarship from the dance program in college. No one expected me to rise up to the top, but the year before graduation, we got a new director. He had just moved to Montreal from France, and he loved contemporary ballet. At the end of the year, I asked the director to let us perform our "Major Freak-Out" duet in one of the smaller performance venues. He agreed to let us do it, and when he saw the piece himself, he fell in love with it—so much so that he subsequently asked us to perform it in other venues to represent the school. It was quite the unexpected way to walk away from a school that at one point I could hardly keep up with.

The performance of "Major Freak Out" was a turning point for me.

Somehow the time I spent keeping up my own expressive voice as I was building my foundation in classical ballet finally paid off. Suddenly, our ability to translate these hours spent in the studio into a substantial piece made my dance partner and I look pretty accomplished in our understanding and interpretation of the art form. It wasn't the first time that expressing myself in my own way had opened new doors for me. It is worth taking a chance and being real about who we are. That's what brought me to this next rule.

Golden Rule 6
Find Your Own Natural Movement

There is something magical about being able to express emotions through the moving body. It is something that can be very healing and done as a practice: putting on music, letting the body just get loose, and following the flow. It also becomes an art form. Teaching dance is teaching the language of dance, but the dance within is already there: it is ourselves manifested through movement.

I believe that without a connection to our emotional self, our soul, and our own inner energy, moving does not have the same power of impact when used for performance and entertainment. Dance needs to be filled with the person's real emotions in order to be effective. Therefore, the person who is dancing needs to stay in touch with that essence, the emotions, and continue to build their own personal connection to dance.

Exploring the emotions that fill us constantly and expressing them in movement connects ourselves to the practice or art of dancing. It's something that needs to be practiced parallel to the training of the dance vocabulary. It's the combination of both together that will make an extraordinary dancer. The technique alone does not have expressive values. It is impressive, of course, but in order for a soul to be touched, the other person's soul has to be there as well. My experience is that by allowing myself time to explore movement on my own, I am able to express myself through dance in a much more meaningful way.

As instructors, we can create time and space for dancers to explore movement in this way. It may be as simple as inviting dancers to choreograph for themselves for a concert or invite them to create a few counts of eight in a class of something that they feel confident practicing. It is easier to cultivate this natural instinct of creating movement at a young age. If a young dancer has built the habit of connecting with their own creative/expressive side, it will be a lot easier for them to keep flowing in their teenage years and beyond

students on stage.

Chapter 7: Avant Premiere [Dress Rehearsal]

Traveling Away

I graduated from college with the performance prize, which acted as a scholarship to fund a trip to France, which then turned into a small tour of several of France's most avant-garde ballet companies. I stayed in France for about six weeks, traveling from one company to the next. My school took this opportunity to promote their program in France by sending me, a graduating student, to visit, take classes, and audition for these companies. It was a great opportunity, and I learned so much.

I remember trudging through the streets of Paris with my big suitcase; I had just arrived in France, 18 years of age. The suitcase anchored me down, yet without it, I would probably have been flying. I remember that first day, taking an aperitif with the people who agreed to host me in Paris. We were on the rooftop of the building right in the center of Montmartre. All I could see were rooftops, and all I could think of was that this was heaven. Being on the road like this, away from Montreal, I felt like I could be whoever I wanted to be. I realized then that I was the only one holding me back. The trip allowed me to take a step into the unknown, and I was going for it.

I saw a lot of great dancing, met wonderful people, and ate delicious food. I networked with many talented dancers, directors, and chore-ographers. I even got an offer to join a company in Lyon, France, but I wasn't ready to settle and not ready to commit just yet. I was in the middle of it all, sent by some of the top people in the dance world to experience some of the most avant-garde work I had ever seen. My mind was blown. I loved everything about traveling. I loved every-thing about France.

Returning Home One Last Time

Upon my return, my dad picked me up at the airport. His presence there should have told me that something was off; I learned he was there with bad news: my brother, the one I promised I would never let anything happen to, had a brain tumor.

After having terrible headaches for a while, he was finally diagnosed: he had a large tumor in the memory area of his brain. Why? Why him? Why now? Why his brain? Why the memory? I was so angry.

When I got back home, as soon as the door to my room closed behind me, I lost it. I was mad. God could go to hell. Everything had been going so well: my dancing was at its peak, I felt terrific physically and mentally, and I was due to return to the company just in time to perform in the "Nutcracker." I thought that life was finally going to be easier, and I felt so encouraged by the all the positive events that had taken place the last few months.

Losing a brother when you are a child makes you feel as though fun is prohibited. You learn early on that life is going to end, and fun seems very futile. When I was seven, I would watch other kids play, and I would think, they don't have a clue. That was a feeling I thought I had finally put aside years after my brother's death. Instead, I was 18, I was just having a little bit of fun, and I felt I was being punished for it.

I returned to the company. Nothing could be done for my brother right away; they had to wait and see if the tumor grew before deciding whether to remove it surgically. So, we waited.

In the meantime, I was invited to choreograph the company's "Emerging Choreographer" concert. I continued at first as though everything was the same, but it started to get harder and harder. I spent a lot of time in the studio, but there was a weight in my heart that I couldn't shake off. I performed a lot, but it felt unfulfilling. I felt disconnected, as though I were missing the connection to dance I had always felt before. Dance was now all business: make rehearsals quick and get right to the stage; it was all so sterile. It felt empty.

On top of everything else, I was not impressed with the company's lifestyle; it didn't seem healthy. There were addictions that I hadn't been exposed to before. There were ways of getting further up in the company by acting in certain ways with the directors, and I didn't like that either. My idea of living as a classical ballet dancer was not turning out the way I had expected.

I was just going through the motions. The intensity of what was going on inside me made everything else seem irrelevant.

The Surgery

Everyone in the family became very anxious when we learned that my brother would have to have surgery to remove his tumor. It was not going to be a simple procedure, and we were all scared about all the possible outcomes. His tumor had grown rapidly, and it had to be removed immediately. The surgery was risky, but the risk of not doing it was even worse. Plus, he was in pain, and there was nothing else they could do for him.

It felt like a replay of past events from my childhood. When my little brother passed away, my mom had unusual reactions: instead of dealing with what admittedly was a difficult reality, she started telling everyone she knew—or anyone who would listen—that she was "finally" discovering herself. At the funeral home, my mom was telling everyone about her newfound love with her music teacher while my little brother was there in his coffin.

Now, 13 years later, we were dealing with my other brother's surgery, and my mom was constantly talking about falling in love with her therapist and consequently being heartbroken. I didn't think it was appropriate that my mom was talking about her attractions to her music teacher years before or her therapist now, but I can understand that reality is hard to deal with sometimes. Stresses made her derail. My mom was never someone I could rely or lean on. She leaned on me plenty, but if I tried leaning on her at any point of my upbringing, I probably would have woken up at the bottom of a ravine.

My brother and I went cross-country skiing one weekend with my mother when I was about 10. We took a path into the woods, following each other single-file: my mom in front, then my brother, then me. We came to a spot where we heard loud growls, and the trees started to move ahead of us; right there stood a bear. It had been a mild winter, and the bear must have woken up from his hibernation. My mom screamed, "Bear!" and turned around, skiing away in the opposite direction. My brother was about eight, so he couldn't ski away fast enough. In a panic, he got himself caught in his skis and started crying. We ended up leaving his skis and ski shoes on the path while we ran away together, me in ski boots and him just in his socks.

My mom ran straight to a house close by, and eventually my brother and I found which house she went to. The people in the house seemed appalled that my mom didn't know where her children were. The whole situation was alarming. I remember feeling again, that it was all on me. She just couldn't deal with anything when stressful situations occurred, and now, years later, after being overall a lot more stable, she still couldn't deal with reality. She was running away from it. I felt like a bear was about to take my brother, and no one could do anything about it.

When my brother was brought back to his hospital room after the surgery, he was speaking words in the wrong order; he was incoherent and didn't make any sense. Something had gone wrong, and the surgeons had to go back in and perform a second surgery. I think at that point, we were all beside ourselves. Luckily, the second surgery was successful.

In the end, though, the story of my brother's recovery turned out to be quite amazing. He not only emerged from the second surgery completely healthy, but the removal of the tumor gave his brain the space back for his memory functions to return to full capacity.

Before the tumor was discovered, his brain found alternative ways for him to remember things, regardless of the pressure of the tumor on that part of his brain. Always an average student, my brother completed high school, earning neither praise nor shame; his academic career was simply par. After the surgery, however, he decided to return to school to take advanced math and science courses so that he could pursue scientific studies in college.

Today, he has a master's degree in environmental genetics and is in great demand in his field. It seems that once the tumor was removed, his brain regained its ability to retain information the way most of us do, but since his brain developed alternative ways to store information, he now had a superior ability to remember things. Of course, I would have been fine with just getting my brother back to us, healthy and happy; he just happened to surprise us all with a newfound sense of aspiration and drive to achievement.

My brother probably knew he might never fully recover from the surgery, and I am sure he saw his successful operation as a new beginning. We were all warned that he may never again be able to walk, talk, or eat normally; the operation was invasive, to say the least. But, it seems that my brother took this second chance at life and decided to make the best of it. I admire him for that. He still has a great big scar on the side of his skull, but scar or no scar, none of us will ever forget what he went through.

Golden Rule 7
Set Goals

The experience with my brother's illness taught me the importance of goal setting. We don't all get a second chance at life. We all have one life, and the more perspective we gain on it, the more we see how important it is to define our goals so that we can follow through with them.

I implement goal setting in all aspects of dance teaching, whether it's at the beginning or end of a semester, the beginning or end of a class, or the beginning or end of an across-the-floor exercise. Goal setting supports students by putting their minds into a place where they can achieve those goals. If you don't really know what you are aiming for, it is hard to be successful.

A lot of us are afraid to set goals because then we're taking the chance of disappointing ourselves. By learning at a young age to set small, attainable goals, students can learn the power of their minds when it comes to surmounting obstacles. It is a very powerful tool, and it is one of the key elements that helps my students build self-esteem through the study of dance.

I often tell my students to set a goal—for instance, "I am going to do three pirouettes." Think it. Believe it. Do it. All goals start in the mind, and when my students believe they will achieve their goals, they never fail to do just that.

Setting goals in real time gives students a chance to show that they believe in their own skills. Going back to the specific goal centers the mind on the now, where the actions take place. Thoughts move us forward, while emotions move us back; the mind walks us through the now.

The Story of Abigail

A few years ago, one of my students injured herself in class. It was a pretty dramatic injury, and gladly it doesn't happen often. She started dancing just a couple of years before, and being tall and very limber for her age made her a bit more vulnerable than others at times. She had worked very hard to get caught up so she could dance with the girls her own age, and the injury was a real blow to her progress. We were doing Grands Battements in the center, talking about what to focus on while executing the step, and she showed us what not to do, and it ironically resulted in an unwanted incident. Her knee gave out from under her, and she collapsed with her knee cap grotesquely on the side of her leg.

For those of you who have ever dislocated a knee can relate to the pain she was in. I was lucky to have a student's mother, an ER nurse, a phone call away, who assisted me in assisting her. Abigail held on to me for about 20 minutes as we waited for the ambulance to arrive. The rest of the group finished class downstairs with an assistant. It was quite dramatic and so sad. The knee dislocated and ripped part of her ligament.

She had surgery a few weeks later. We were preparing for our annual "Nutcracker" performance, and she knew she was not going to be able to perform as planned. Her mom called me from the hospital when she woke up from the surgery, saying her daughter wanted to talk to me. She wanted to know if I would let her perform in a wheelchair. I had tears in my eyes. "Of course," I said. "You can be the grandmother in the party scene. We'll have you come on stage in your wheelchair." She was so happy, and it made me think. It made me feel how meaningful this all was.

Her daughter came back to rehearsals in her wheelchair a few weeks later, and her spirit was so uplifting. She wanted to be there. She wanted to dance, and somehow nothing was going to be in her way.

She healed well and did a wonderful job rehabbing from the injury, and she is now stronger than she ever was. She performed the following year in full capacity. What a spirit this girl has! And the determination that she showed touched me greatly.

When we want something, nothing can stand in the way of us reaching it, except us feeling that it is unobtainable. Believing that our heart's desire is a possibility is where it all starts. Giving ourselves a chance to succeed or at least try, is priceless. Watching girls like Abigail prove that it is all possible is immensely humbling.

We all have the ability to inspire one another. Setting a goal is believing in ourselves but also in each other, as we need to feel the support of others to expose our most vulnerable wishes out in the open. It takes trust, and that's what builds communities. It forges us as people, but it also brings us closer as we choose to believe that it is all possible and therefore limitless.

Chapter 8: Le Premier Act [The First Act]

Returning to the Ashram

The summer after my brother's surgery, I was invited to do a dance performance at the ashram. I was meant to visit for a weekend, but as I walked into the well-known space so many years later, I knew I had to be there a little while longer, as I was yearning for that connection back within myself. I was in need to realign myself with what I really wanted, and I was ready to give back. I spent a transformational summer there at age 14, and now that I had developed new skills and abilities, I was ready to offer a little back to the place that pretty much saved my life.

Everything fell into place nicely. After only a few days there, I met Chantal, a former stewardess. She told me stories of riding her fast motorcycle through town, with her bum higher than her shoulders, and her hip-length hair pulled back into a braid, whipping in the wind.

We became friends at first sight. Chantal was offering work with the ashram's board of directors on their fundraising campaign that was aiming to restore some of the buildings on the ashram grounds. She was looking for someone to help in the office. Her previous helper returned home, and she asked whether I was interested in joining their team, and I was. It wasn't dance, but it was real, concrete (literally), and different for me. I was excited for something different.

I chose to stay. It wasn't rational, and it wasn't convenient, but it was what my soul yearned for, and I couldn't go against it. I had to leave my life behind for a while to see where that new adventure would take me. I had to dive deeper into the real meaning of my existence, and the first step was to start here, where I once had to bring myself back to love and life again.

Chantal and I quickly became best buddies and spent a lot of our time together. We'd have the best times: chuckling at our desks, twisting in laughter over lunch, and sneaking off the beaten paths likes kids. It certainly felt like finding a sister.

During the same period of time, I joined the leadership program that the ashram had just initiated for the young adults living on-site. The program was open to young adults aged 18 to 30 who had been involved in the spiritual practices for many years. About 25 of us from various countries around the world met up every day to study scriptures and learn how to apply them in our daily lives. We were encouraged to meditate at least an hour every day, and we met one evening a week to discuss our experiences.

It was a wonderful community of people. During the Christmas season, I organized a little performance of "The Nutcracker" with dancers and dance lovers that were living there. It was clear that I had to keep up with my own dancing, and I was able to utilize a little gym that was available for the staff to practice ballet and stretches on my own when I could.

The fundraising campaign that we were conducting was pretty spectacular; it was an international organization with donors from all parts of the world, from newscasters to country singers, actresses, and writers - you name it. We were dealing with donor lists worth millions and throwing fundraising events matching those of the most prestigious art organizations. I had unknowingly stepped into a whole new circle of people. Even though I had been involved in movies, fashion shows, and distinctive events in Montreal while in the dance company and during my training, this was the United States, and it was filled with glamour. I was very proud to be a part of such a dynamic team, and that is where I met my first husband, Phillip.

Phillip was involved at the ashram a bit like me—his family had been bringing him there since he was a child. At 23, he was the youngest campaign donor. I thought that was attractive; it wasn't so much because he had money, but he was already able at a young age to support something other than just himself. After his visit, we started writing to each other. Phillip was born in Moscow and spoke Russian at home. He was a smart young man with a bright future ahead of him.

When I met Phillip, I knew I found a nice man. He was educated but also spiritual; he was strong but gentle; he had a strong path ahead of him and held the ability to wake up and walk that path every day. After a few months writing to each other, we spent Christmas together at the ashram. Then, a few weeks later, we met up in New York City for our first real date.

A month or two after that, I drove back to Boston with him to see his place. I told myself that if I were to find a job in Boston the next day, I was going to stay with Phillip in Boston. By noon the next day, I found a job in Boston. I was going to be one of those kick-ass waitresses in a pub close to the financial district. The fact that I could hardly speak English and could barely take someone's order didn't seem to be an issue to the hiring manager. I didn't even wear a short skirt. I came up with a winning combination of Canadian French and the Russian English I was picking up on; it seemed to work for all the men in suits flooding the pub after work for happy hour.

I moved out of the ashram and in with Phillip into his small apartment in Beacon Hill in Boston. Phillip and I were able to take each other away from the seriousness of daily life with laughter; it was easy. We were constantly entertained by the sheer joy of each other's company. By then, Phillip was a serious 24-year-old man whose work was building mathematical models to minimize risk in stock market portfolios. His models sold all over the world, which required him to travel a lot. During one of his trips, I traveled back to Montreal for a visit with my family and was stopped at the border when I tried to return to the States. I never entered the United States illegally, but now with my lack of plans and lack of an official residence, I realize that I looked suspicious to the immigration officers.

I watched as the authorities emptied and searched each one of my bags. All of my belongings were spilled out onto the ground—cosmetics, lingerie, jeans, books, hair brushes, etc. They sent me back to Canada. I watched the bus drive by, feeling like a fool. They were not letting me back into the United States without a proper visa. Phillip drove through the night and asked me to marry him as the sun rose the next day. It was romantic. All I wanted was to get the hell out of my life and into his. I said yes.

Getting Married

It took three months to get the proper visa to re-enter the country as Phillip's fiancée. We got married in the summer of 1999; I was only 21. We were married a few blocks away from what is now my main dance studio right here on Cape Cod. Life has a crazy way of bringing us back to the same territory.

We had a beautiful, windy wedding on Cape Cod by Scraggy Neck Beach in someone's home right on the water. We asked a well-known preacher from the Bronx, New York, to marry us. We had met him a few times at the ashram, and he drove right from the city for our ceremony. It was a wild wedding in the sense that I had just arrived to the country a few days prior, and we had people from all over the hemisphere attend the wedding. Our guest list was a varied mix of ballet dancers, stock brokers, financial analysts, artists, family, friends, and others. The stock of wine and beer was emptied halfway through the night despite ordering twice as much as the caterer suggested. A party of Russians and Canadians will do that, and everyone was still talking about the ballerinas going skinny dipping a few years after the event—that's Cape Cod for you.

Married life turned out to be like everything else: not exactly what I was expecting. Living with Phillip in Boston for a couple of months was different from what it was like when I officially entered Phillip's family. There were cultural differences that neither of us could have anticipated. Phillip grew up in a very close-knit Russian family and was especially close to his mom. The first time I saw him and his mother together, I was shocked. They curled up together on the couch like little animals, and he started to cry softly because he was so happy to see her. I wanted to puke.

Being emotional is admirable more often than not, but I think that there are times when being emotional does not help. It turned out that my first husband was a crybaby. He would cry once or twice a week for no apparent reason: he cried because the food was so good, he cried because he was so happy, he cried because he was overwhelmed with mixed emotions -- anything could trigger his tears. When he cried, I would be internally rolling my eyes as I watched him. I spent many years building up defense mechanisms against most of my emotions to make sure I could function well in this world. Phillip was surfing the ups and downs of each one of his emotions, and I was getting seasick.

Because I didn't contribute as much financially as Phillip did, and since I had never been used to speaking up during my childhood and adolescence, I went along with what my husband thought was the right thing to do. I wouldn't say I was passive, but in some ways, perhaps I was passive by default. Immigration is a long process, even when you are moving to and from a neighboring country. I had to get used to the US system and get my own papers in order. To be honest, I was somewhat uncomfortable by the fact that I couldn't do more for our relationship, but I was overwhelmed by all the changes. I couldn't hold a conversation on the phone with anyone because of the language barrier and had trouble expressing myself eloquently. I had to

guess what most people were saying to me even in person. I wanted to contribute more to our new life together, but I felt limited with what I could do.

The ashram had been a microcosm in a way; being with a lot of people from different areas of the world, it was understood that everyone spoke different languages. In the real world, the language was fast, and the street talk was different from what I was used to. I hadn't really heard and used many swear words in English by then. I remember practicing for over a week what I heard the pub owner say to someone at work, just to get the hang of it. "Get the hell out of here." I just tried it again, and it still doesn't sound right. Oh well.

A few months after moving to Boston, I started dancing with a local company. I started doing fundraising work for a perform-ing arts space. I gathered a group of artists that would come togeth-er to brainstorm and get ideas from one another. At that time, Phillip and I had a great loft space right on Massachusetts Avenue near Harvard Square, so it was a great spot to bring people over and network.

Phillip and I moved often, as he was always seeking new scenarios, exploring life-styles, and work opportunities. Phillip was pulled between wanting to work in the financial industry and also wanting to be a musician. During our two years in the Boston area, we lived in Beacon Hill, the loft in Cambridge, and then commuted from his parents' house on Cape Cod; after all that, we ended up buying a loft across the water from the financial district. A few months later, we put it back on the market when we ultimately decided to move to New York.

Phillip was unhappy. He felt divided, as though the two parts of him were in conflict. I had trouble understanding how he felt. To me, Phillip seemed to have the best of both worlds: he could make money during the day and express himself through music at night and on the weekends. Most artists would love to have a day job that pays a six-figure salary in their early 20s. Even now, I have been running a dance studio for over 10 years, and I have never felt confused about where the artist begins and the businesswoman ends or vice versa. To me, it feels as though I'm still just one person trying to make things work. I didn't love Phillip any less due to my difficulties understanding him, but I had trouble finding ways to help him. In the meantime, it was hard for me to really build something of my own since we kept changing locations and lifestyles. Since I was new to the whole world around me, I was probably more affected by it than Phillip was. It seemed to always shift, and I had trouble creating something substantial.

Phillip and I decided to move to the New York City area when his dad opened his own company in Montclair, New Jersey, performing work related to finance. As his mother was also opening a new business, a center for well-being, I thought it would be a good time to get closer to his family. I thought this move could be more permanent this time, so I was excited about it. I honestly thought it would be nice for the two of us to support his parents in their business ventures. I am always interested in hearing about business, seeing it come through, and watching it grow. What I didn't realize, however, was that I was walking into a family with its own unique sets of rules.

I didn't always feel included, and since I already experienced the feeling of rejection from my own family, it didn't take much for that well-known feeling to resurface. Basically, working with Phillip's mother didn't work out for long. I think she really wanted to work with her own daughter, not me.

It soon seemed like a good idea to find a job elsewhere, and soon enough, I found a job right in Union Square in New York City, assisting the director of an international art organization in their capital campaign. I started commuting every day to and from the city. Eventually, I found my own little apartment by Washington Square in Manhattan. I was slowly taking myself out of the family the way I knew best. It just seemed like the most normal thing for me to do: stand on the outside of the family circle.

Family was an issue in our marriage from early on. For our honeymoon, we had planned to spend two extra nights in a B&B on the Cape after the wedding, but we ended up cutting the trip short. His mother wanted to see Phillip before they left, and his sister wanted to talk to me about something that happened at the wedding. So, we drove back. I couldn't understand why his parents were so pushy about it. They lived just an hour away. My family and friends traveled all the way from Canada, yet no one on my side expected to see us or even talk to us the next day.

Phillip insisted we had to see his parents as they requested, and it was awkward. His sister made a cake that was meant for us to cut at the wedding, but we didn't, which made her sad. I felt bad, but I didn't even know about her cake, and I just didn't feel as responsible as they made me feel for her breakdown. It made me feel just like I used to in my own father's house as a child: unwelcomed, troublesome, and unimportant.

I would probably deal with his sister better now, but it was so much to handle then. On the wedding day, the hairdresser lost it on me because she didn't know it was my actual wedding day and refused to do my hair in fear of not doing something I would be happy with. My mom and brother got into a small car accident on their way in from Canada, and they arrived late. Honestly, it was a little rushed since I had just arrived in the country three days prior to the wedding. Phillip's sister's cake was the last thing on my mind, and her breakdown was insignificant compared to all the other life-changing events that were going on elsewhere in my life.

I blame his mother a lot for our breakup. After Philip and I separated, I told her nicely that I never had a chance to be a wife to him because she'd never taken her tentacles off him. I asked her to give him some space for his future wife's sake. I never had the stamina, the self-confidence, or the desire to fight her for him; I left enough behind to be with him. I expected our marriage to be a done deal, and I was never going to be the type of woman to impose myself or my needs on my partner. His mother was doing all the bossing around that one man could take. I became the one he turned to for support. Eventually, that changed the dynamic and the nature of our relationship.

I met Phillip's future girlfriend a few months after our separation. She was a girl from Poland and spoke some Russian; Phillip's mother already met her. The three of us had dinner, then they officially started dating. I actually liked her a lot. She asked me if there was any chance of Phillip and me getting back together, and she inquired if it was okay with me if she dated him. She didn't have to do that, but I thought it was a nice gesture. I appreciated her candor, and because she was asserting herself in her new role in Phillip's life in a very well-mannered way, all I wanted to show moving forward was support. We had a great time that night, and to this day, it makes me happy to know that he is with someone nice.

I have worked with a lot of women, and I do believe that women can become overly competitive when it comes to work, self-worth, and territory. Auditioning in New York City was an eye-opener. By then, I auditioned in many places—not just in Montreal, but also in locations in France, Switzerland, Belgium, Holland, and Germany. New York City female dancers are vicious, and the atmosphere in the corridors outside of dance studios was cutthroat and vindictive. I am not exaggerating when I say that other women shot me looks that could have killed. I knew that money could be tight in such an expensive city, and the competition for roles were fierce, but I just wanted to say to them, *Lets bring it down a notch, shall we?*

Golden Rule: 8
Competition Should Never Lead to Hatred

I was always and still am very competitive. I have no problem with competition—it keeps me on my toes. As long as competition is healthy and stimulating, it should be accepted and supported. Sometimes, however, it can cross a line. This has become one of my rules in teaching dance: competition should never lead to hatred.

In my dance teaching, I believe that when a student gets upset with someone other than herself, the competition has gone too far. Competition is a great way to keep the level of energy high in a class, which is probably true in an office as well. When we focus our competitiveness on ourselves, we push ourselves to achieve our own goals, not somebody else's.

When I started owning a business on Cape Cod, I was exposed to other types of rivalry. Surprisingly, at least in the area, dance studios can get pretty competitive, and it can be disconcerting at times. I had to learn to keep my focus on myself and what I was trying to do with my business. It can easily take one's focus away from the real meaning of what one is trying to accomplish.

A rival studio owner reached out to one of my instructors, years ago, and convinced her to work at her studio. The instructor had been teaching for me for about two years at the time, instructing a few days each week and helping in the office as well, so she had all of my students' contact information. The offer must have been good, and not knowing anything about their conversation, I was taken aback when she announced her departure only a month and a half before our holiday show. She was leaving choreographies with her students unfinished and leaving me stranded in a time of year where it is almost impossible to find replacement.

It's fair to say I was upset and even more so when I heard from students at the time that she'd been making calls to have students follow her to the other studio. It didn't cause any real damage in terms of business, but I remember feeling that it was a level of competition I was uncomfortable with. The other studio owner ended up firing the instructor who had left my studio to teach at hers, at the end of the school year, and I was genuinely saddened by what she had done. I felt she had bribed a young woman into doing something that was not ethical and did not have her back at the end of the day.

The Indian scriptures talk about dharmic wars that are fought with righteousness. It is referred as Dharma-yuddha, a Sanskrit word made up of two roots: Dharma meaning "righteousness," and yuddha meaning "warfare." In the ancient Indian texts, dharma-yuddha refers to a war that is fought while following several rules that make the war fair.

The Mahabharata epic, for example, is an old Sanskrit poem which describes the Kurukshetra war: the two sides agree on a set of rules to uphold the principles of righteousness. For instance, equals fight equals, and the buildup of weapons and armies is done with the full knowledge of the opposing side and no surprise attacks are made.

The rules of engagement also set out how warriors were to deal with noncombatants. No one should attack an enemy who has temporarily lost or dropped their weapon. The lives of women, prisoners of war, and farmers were also sacred. Pillaging the land was forbidden, and the dharma-yuddha also signified that the war was not to be fought for gain or selfish reasons.

We may live in a different time now, but it is important to remember that there are basic rules in life that are important to follow. Otherwise, it is just a free-for-all. All the problems with bullying is a result from forgetting basic etiquettes of life.

What I like about those texts is that they embrace the reality of competition or war between people, but they also remind us that there is a way to do it righteously and with respect.

In the classroom, it means this: no eye rolling, no undermining comments, no judgements, and no verbal or non-verbal comparison of one another. This sadly has to start at the top, which means, with the instructors. Adults are just as guilty of engaging in cutting behaviors.

We have an amazing opportunity to create a space where students can learn to fight their own battles in the classroom and learn to reach to their goals with the help and support of the group. Even the smallest remarks can alter the sense of safety that is so important to maintain for healthy expansion to take place. Watch that the dance floor remains a place of fairness for everyone to be in. Don't let competition lead to hatred. Remind everyone that respecting everyone for who they are is the righteous way to be.

students backstage

Chapter 9: L'Entre-Act [The Intermission]

New York City

When Phillip and I were in the Boston area, I danced with an acrobatic dance troupe that created work collaboratively. In spite of all the body bruises, we certainly had a blast. I was never one to walk on my hands, but somehow I found myself upside down, balancing on my elbows and head—mine as well as others'. I was pushing my fears away by acquiring new levels of physical strength and discovering new capabilities to what my body could do. As a troupe, we were also pushing the edge with our performances.

When Phillip and I decided to move to New York City, I continued to push my body's limit through yoga. I was taking yoga classes three to four times a week in a studio where the room was kept really warm. These classes pushed my body to new levels of flexibility and strength. I started creating solo routines that I performed live or captured on film in the city or even in nature. Although I was performing in a way that was more in line with my artistic point of view, I still continued to seek something else, something new.

Although there were many wonderful things happening in my life, I still had the feeling that there was something else I had to do, and I couldn't figure out what it was. It was making me anxious. At the time, Phillip and I had two separate spaces to live, but we still spent most of our time together. After a few months, I started having difficulty sleeping and started yearning for some time apart. I needed time and space for my soul to talk to me.

Then September 11th happened. I was alone in the apartment on Thompson Street when the planes hit the two towers. I remember going outside on the street and seeing chaos. And there, just a few

steps away in Washington Square, I saw the towers crumble, and every single person present fell on their knees. It was unbelievable. I stayed in the city for the rest of the day, trying to find a way to get off the island to join Phillip who was in Montclair working with his father. But I was stuck for a while, like everyone else, unable to leave Manhattan. It was an immensely difficult day for thousands of people. Since Phillip worked in the financial industry for years, he knew many people who worked in the twin towers.

By the time I reached him by train back in New Jersey, he already made the decision to move again, and I was ready to follow him. Again.

Two years after getting married, Phillip and I decided to move back to the Cape. Phillip wanted to change his career, and though I was fulfilled with what I was doing, I was also happy to step away from New York City for a little while. I had to decide the morning of the attack whether I would hold onto the lease of my apartment. The next day, Phillip and I emptied the place and left for Cape Cod.

I loved being on the Cape again. Having lived in cities all my life, I was most impressed by the occasional sighting of a fox or a coyote. I loved the hawks, the ravens, the owls, and the deer. I felt like I started to breathe again, and soon we knew we had to make a change in our relationship.

Breaking up was a mutual decision. He didn't want to stay on the Cape, and I wasn't ready to move again. Since I left Montreal, we had moved every six months, and it was getting to me. Phillip liked things to move fast, yet it seemed that every time I was starting to settle in somewhere, making friends and getting projects underway, he was ready to make a move again. So I stayed on the Cape, and he left. He now lives in Europe. We haven't seen much of each other since. We turned the page on a beautiful chapter of our lives.

I often wonder how I ended up living on the Cape. Simply enough, I came with someone, he left, and I stayed. There were a lot of teaching opportunities for me on the Cape, I loved the ocean, and I wanted peace. And peace is what I found.

Finding My Own Creative Path

The morning after Phillip left, I found an open nut right in front of the back door; it was probably blown there by the wind, but I took it as a sign that nature was welcoming me to this place. Soon, I was reconnecting with my own creative energy. I was painting, singing, and playing the piano again. I began forming ideas on creativity and thinking about ways to teach it through dance.

I realized that there was a message I was eager to get out. I wanted to build a new set of rules—rules about love, rules about taking care of one another, rules about expression, and rules about how to encourage people to express themselves in a creative way. I wanted to start a revolution.

I had no credit card, no credit history, and no savings account. I didn't feel Phillip deserved for me to tie him down financially because of our marriage. I had a few boxes, a lot of ambitions, and almost spoke English by then. I was scared, but I was happy.

I was connecting with my own creative flow, and I was learning to distinguish it from the learning of a craft. I started seeing creativity as an art that goes beyond the art forms. I started to see that the art is a method of assembling things in a way that satisfies our souls without overthinking the results, standards, or opinions. I began to realize how the simple time spent creating something out of nothing was vital

for all of our equilibrium. I was just learning that we have to let our creative energy flow and to let our soul shine through.

Arts and all creative endeavors help us stay connected to the parts of ourselves that are often forgotten. Any creative activity can bring us that sense of accomplishment that we so crave for. As I found myself alone on the Cape, I was ready to get busy doing something that would have real meaning in my life. I had to find my mission and start my own revolution.

After finding a space where I could be creative in a safe environment back on the Cape, I discovered my sacred space back in the dance studio. There, I found my calling: I was going to teach.

I started teaching classical ballet a few nights a week, and I quickly expanded my dance teaching to several schools. The number of my students kept growing in each of the studios. The students were hungry for new creative projects, and they were open to new choreographic ideas.

Within six months, I was teaching six days a week in four different studios. With students ranging in age from three years old to 75, I found different ways to relate to each age group and communicate my love of dance with each one. It was the beginning of something beautiful.

experimenting with watercolors

Golden Rule 9
Learn by Teaching Others

My experience with dance deepened to a whole new level when I started to teach. Communicating with others forced me to really grab on to the knowledge that was inside of me. Until I started sharing my love of dance and my love for the art form, I didn't really realize how much I cared and how much I had to share. It was very empowering and very fulfilling.

This has been true for my students as well. When I see my older students coach or assist me in class, they are deepening their own understanding and love for dance, too. Young students take great pride in teaching their parents and siblings what they learned in class. As I mentioned earlier, children are compelled to know everything about something, not just a small portion of things. They want to be able to soak up the information and make it their own so that when they think about it, they can make sense of it. Time and time again I have learned, as a teacher that I can't share anything with my students before thoroughly grasping it myself, and their own internal process in assimilating the information is the same.

Teaching provides dancers the opportunity to enhance their own understanding. A lot of the students will assist me with other classes. Every student who has taken the opportunity to step into the classroom as an assistant has made great progress in his or her own training. The process of teaching is an important step for students in building their self-esteem and strengthening their understanding of the art form. I think it's very empowering for students to realize how much they have learned and how much they know. For the parents, too, it's nice for them to see that what their kids have studied for so many years can be passed on to others.

The Story of a Lost Teacher

I lost one of my instructors recently. We had just begun the semester, and we tried to adjust things in the curriculum of her program when she decided it was time for her to go. I had a difficult time finding someone to replace her with such short notice. I couldn't find her replacement, and it got me thinking: I simply had to find a solution. You know when things don't flow, and you have to stop and think, what is it? I received a call from one of the mothers. Her daughter had been taking classes with me for years in the ballet and jazz program, and she said, "You know, my daughter would love to help you teach in the jazz program." And it kind of clicked.

I have been talking about building self-esteem, and at that moment I had the opportunity to take this to the next level. I thought to myself that I can guide the older students in teaching the younger kids' classes. They will be supervised, I can build a curriculum with them, and somehow, I knew this was going to give my older girls an opportunity to really grow into not only the dancers they want to be, but the young models that they are for the studio. We restructured part of the program so that some of the younger groups were going to be taught by the advanced dancers at the studio, and the results were great.

This opportunity for the older students to not only teach but also create choreography for the younger dancers has brought together many of the elements that help dancers flourish. It nourishes both the older students' need to affirm their knowledge and find their creative voices; the younger dancers could then find role models that would help define their own goals for the future.

I've had many teachers over the years, and this recent model as helped me, as a studio owner, see the importance of building a solid curriculum for the school in all the programs. I have had the privilege of having very talented dancers/teachers instruct at the studio over the years, but I have also come to recognize that the curriculum is just as important as the person teaching the class.

Over the years, it has become clear to me that having a structured curriculum is key to homogeneity in the teaching of a program. Consistency and precision is very important, and I feel this new step has helped define our school even more. This new structure empowers the instructor, and it creates a platform for younger teachers to come in as faculty without feeling like the world is on their shoulders. They have resources, they have guidance, and they can succeed doing something that is really helpful to them and to the younger dancers.

So, yes, let dancers deepen their own understanding and experiences of dance by teaching back. It's a beautiful thing. Guide them, and help them be successful. You will see the circle created by letting students teach in a way that is supported by a curriculum that creates growth on so many levels.

Chapter 10: Le Deuxième Act [The Second Act]

Teaching Dance on Cape Cod

It was great to be on Cape Cod; I felt engaged and loved, and everything seemed to be falling into place. I met wonderful young dancers and started doing projects with students from the different studios. I was happy to be not only teaching dance but also helping to create a network of like-minded people. I then met Diane, who owned a studio in Chatham. Diane was in her late 50s. She had decided to pursue her passion for dance later in life and opened a dance studio after successfully running a business in town for most of her life. She was dedicated, and her artistic point of view in regard to dance and dance education was close to mine.

Diane's dance studio was structured as a not-for-profit organization, raising money for a scholarship fund to pay for dance education for kids who could not afford to take classes. Sometimes the money was also used toward paying the tuition of talented dancers who might not have been able to continue their dance education in college.

I started teaching for Diane one day a week in January 2002. I would often stay over in Chatham after my classes and spend time with her and her husband in their beautiful home. We became fast friends. My previous experiences working for the director's capital campaign fundraising at the ashram, and in NYC as the executive assistant to the director of an international art organization, gave me good credentials. So when I met Diane, I had experience with her type of business so that I could really make a contribution to it. I understood the needs and requirements of a not-for-profit, and I became pretty good at fundraising and donor management. Working with Diane and her organization was one way to bridge the two sides of my professional life.

Diane was a wonderful woman to learn business from; she knew her stuff, and she had built a nice life for herself. I was impressed by her success.

After she and I spent a few months together in the winter and spring, Diane asked me to run her studio for the summer. I was honored for the opportunity, and I moved a bit closer to Chatham to avoid dealing with the summer tourist traffic. I realized then that running a dance studio could be rather fun, and being successful at it was empowering. I also realized that I liked the idea of owning a small business.

Somehow things were starting to come together. As a classical ballet teacher, I felt I was on solid ground. I felt confident in what I knew. At the same time, I spent the last few years trying to find a different way to connect with dance, taking many different turns. I left the dance company to do a leadership program at the ashram; I worked in f undraising for two charitable organizations; I danced with other troupes and on my own. Now things were starting to come together and make sense.

Dance was my medium. I devoted many years to building myself as a dancer, both physically and emotionally. I began to think of classical ballet as my language, the form through which I could communicate, expressing my own voice. And that is when Form, Focus, and Energy came in.

Golden Rule 10
Find Form, Focus, Energy

I was in the classroom one day teaching, and it came to me like a mantra: Form, Focus, Engergy. Dancers need form—the body needs to be physically capable of holding a position without excess tension. Form is empty, however, without focus, the quality of being present in the moment. And finally, it is energy that allows our own spirited self to manifest through movement.

Form, focus, and energy. This is the mantra I use now in class. The silence of the form, the focus of the mind, and the enthusiasm in one's own energy.

Whether at the beginning of an exercise or as we get prepared for an event, we need these three elements: form, focus, energy. It is true in rehearsals that as a group and individually, we prepare ourselves as dancers to give our best performance. We need to remind ourselves to build on all three levels: the form applies to the body and finding that neutral ground to start from, focus comes from the mind being in the present moment, and energy is the self—the vital energy inside each one of us that defines us, keeps us real and expressive, and committed to the now.

This is primordial in teaching and in life as well. I believe having all three elements present in our life will bring us great happiness. Sometimes we have the form, we have a beautiful life, a home, a family, and a career; we may have the stamina and the mental focus to make everything work well every day; but without our own passion, our loving what we do, and our enthusiasm, it will be hard to be completely fulfilled in the life that we have.

On the other hand, we can have great focus and great clarity of the mind; we can have passion, enthusiasm, and drive; but without the form, whether it is the opportunity for work, education or other basic elements, like our health, or bodily strength holding us back, it will be hard to fulfill our heart's desire.

dancer at the barre

Similarly, lack of focus or the ability to stop and enjoy the moment, can also create setbacks or lack of real joy.

I believe we need all three, form, focus, and energy, to succeed at being really happy in our life. We need all three.

Form:
Make sure to support your body so it is ready to support you in your endeavor; make sure your home is a safe place for you to come back to; make sure your work is a place where you feel you can truly accomplish yourself; make sure your family is a place for you to grow as a person and feel nurtured.

Focus:
Make sure you mind is clear, present to what you are doing; make sure that your intentions are clear, fluid and in harmony with each other; make sure your goals are defined and out in the open; most important-ly, make sure that your attention is here in the now.

Energy:
Make sure you can connect to that vital energy inside yourself that you know what is it that makes your heart sing, what fires you up with love, commitment, and enthusiasm. Make sure you know what you care most about and that you align yourself with that every day so that your daily actions express that vital energy that the heart ignites .

It is simple in a way, and it is also not. We all get busy and carried away with everyday life, but we have to give ourselves a chance to succeed at life, and by that, I mean we must find our own happiness.

Chapter 11: Le Troisième Act [The Third Act]

Becoming a Business Owner

In my second year on Cape Cod, I started co-directing the studio in Chatham with Diane. I was commuting a little over 45 minutes each way in the car. I didn't really mind it, as commuting allowed me to return calls before I got to the office and started working. I remember going home over the holidays that year and telling my dad: "My life is good—I just wish the studio was right down the street from where I live."

Ironically, when I came back to Cape Cod for the First Night performance, I got a call from a woman who I didn't know personally, but she had heard about me and was calling to offer me her dance school business. The location of the school was less than a mile down the street from where I lived – talk about getting what you wish for! I only had just about a week to make a decision. Classes resumed for the new session in a couple of weeks, and because of my already busy schedule, I needed time to make everything work. I had already committed to teaching at and co-directing the dance studio in Chatham, and I was still teaching at the other studio as well.

What was I going to say? Sorry, I changed my mind. I don't really want to work right down the street. I didn't want to take my luck for granted, and it sure did feel like destiny. So I agreed to take over the business.

Diane wasn't thrilled about the new business offer. My first instinct had been to have the new studio be part of her business, but she was not interested in that kind of expansion. Diane's studio was not busy enough to support having me there more than a few days a week, so adding another location closer to me made sense. As with most things at that time, she and I weren't seeing eye-to-eye, but I knew I had to keep going forward, and if she didn't want to expand with me, I had to do it alone. She actually threw me out of her house that day. Maybe she was sad at the thought of me being less involved, but I still didn't like the feeling. I finished the year teaching and co-directing her studio regardless of my new responsibilities in fairness for the opportunity she had given me.

The new business came with students. I had approximately 20 hours of teaching to do at the new studio, 10 hours in Chatham, and four hours at the other studio; add in 10 hours of commuting per week, two schools to oversee, and three recitals to prepare. It was intense, but I liked where things were going.

It's in that period of time that I met Brad. Getting to know Brad was a slow process; he taught guitar next door to one of the four studios I had started teaching at when I first arrived on Cape. I was teaching ballet, and he and I ended our lessons at the same time one day a week, and after a few months, we started hanging out after work in a pizza joint in town. Brad was mellow, and I found his calmness contagious. That calmness could easily be mistaken for depth, but I never really found out if it was or wasn't. Since he was a bit withdrawn, he gave me a bit of blank canvas on which I could create a whole character for him. He was hard to get to know, but I liked that. It made him interesting.

Brad played in a band and taught music on the side. He was a no-nonsense kind of guy. As the son of a minister, Brad grew up with church in his home. I found out through the years that that defined him a lot more than I thought it would and not for the reasons I would have guessed. He was sensitive to the meaning of goodness, but I think at times he was also rebelling against goodness.

The best part of our relationship was that we supported each other in our business ventures, as we both needed a bit of reassurance and maybe a little encouragement. There was something non-threatening about our relationship that allowed me to focus most of my energy on expanding my professional life. Our lives became more and more intertwined over the first four years of our relationship.

Brad opened his own shop, so we were both moving forward and getting more and more involved in teaching. We built our businesses side by side and started helping each other in the pursuit of our own dreams. He was a big part of my being able to get the studio to where it is now. There was a big learning curve to go through when it came to producing shows to the caliber that we do now, and taking over the studio close to home also meant I was going to start producing the annual Nutcracker in the area. Brad was the other half of the team when it came to deal with the tech at the theater and dealing with the extensive sceneries and costumes that I purchased from the previous owner.

We learned to work hard side by side doing things that we both loved and cared about. It was at the heart of our relationship to help each other go after our dreams and make it a reality. And that taught me about the meaning of discipline. We weren't just helping each other get things done. We were helping each other discover our own callings, and that was bringing us closer to a life filled with integrity, with discipline.

dancer on stage

Golden Rule 11
Practice Discipline

Discipline—such a popular topic! I have listened to and read many ideas, opinions, and suggestions about discipline in dance training, yoga, spiritual practices, and in everyday life.

We discuss discipline often in dance training, as it is extremely regimented. When I think of the emotional, spiritual nature of discipline, I also feel it means to have the mindfulness and awareness to be present with our self on a moment-to-moment basis. Not in a r egimented way but with awareness. Be well. Do what makes you happy. Be full of joy. Live with enthusiasm. Stop when it's too much. Do more of something when you crave it. Go after your goal. Be a better person. Don't stop or go just because. Know what your heart wants. Be in tune with the song that resonates inside your soul. Listen to yourself. This is all discipline to me.

When we discipline ourselves to do what makes us truly happy, we're not only in a better mood, but we also do nicer things for other people, who then do nicer things for other people. At the end of the day, because we have taken the time to practice discipline over our life by listening to our heart's true desire, we have helped others have a better day as well. The influence of that day can spread over a week, the week over a month, and so on. Discipline within ourselves can spread goodness rapidly and widely.

Practically everyone has an opinion about how to achieve self-im-provement, but in the end, actions speak louder than words, and our state of being speaks louder than actions. I don't want to be judged, and I don't expect anyone to want to be judged by me or anyone else. I don't feel that God is disappointed with me if I don't do this or that. The universe opens when my heart does, and my heart opens when I remember to take good care of it.

My job is to keep my heart open and to stay in line with what triggers its enthusiasm, what fuels its fire, gives me energy, and inspires me to move forward with love.

True changes happen when there is love: self-love and the love and tenderness towards and from others. Discipline is not a dry form to adhere to, but it's a state of mind that creates real potential for change. Once a real goal has been set in motion because of a spark of interest or an intention, discipline arrives as a vessel to carry us to it, but it is alive only by our determination and passion. Hard work is a beautiful thing, and we all know it is needed to succeed in the face of adversity; it should be fueled by a commitment that is tangible in our hearts.

I hate to follow rules I don't understand or ones that no one ever bothered to explain to me. In my dance teaching, I don't arbitrarily impose rules: instead, I help my students think about discipline as a decision to make the best out of their lives. Without such a decision, time is lost, energies are depleted, momentum is stalled, and life can careen out of control.

When the heart knows its purpose and the mind has set its agenda, discipline is everyone's best friend.

I practice discipline over my choices so that I can remember to choose to love rather than judge, to breathe rather than tense up, to open up rather than resist, and to be myself rather than what others want me to be.

When everyone involved in a dance class, a performance, or a re-hearsal understands the goal of what we are here to do, the practice of discipline becomes automatic. The understanding and acceptance of a common objective rallies every participant. Discipline becomes alive as a reaffirmation of a goal, rather than a restriction, a punishment, or an exemption of power.

The best way to teach discipline is to help students reaffirm their goals and support each other in being true to ourselves always because really, that is what dance is all about.

dancers backstage

Chapter 12: L'apothéose [The Apotheosis]

My Second Honeymoon

I persuaded Brad to marry me as I was walking out the door four years after we started dating. I wanted things to become more settled as our lives became more filled with responsibilities. We got engaged, we bought a house, and we stayed engaged for a little over three years. Before the end of the fourth year of our engagement, we ran to City Hall in Boston to get married.

The wedding took about 10 minutes. It was kind of rebellious and fun. Four days later, Brad totaled my car—not in a car accident or any kind of life-threatening situation but by going through a puddle. I kept telling him that my car wouldn't make it through that puddle, that it was too deep, but he was annoyed with me, and he didn't want to listen to me anymore. I told him he was driving my car, so he had to. Next thing you know, the car died in the middle of the puddle. We walked out of the car, and that was pretty much it. I couldn't even look at him for a whole day after that.

This didn't feel like a good start to our married life. I loved my car, and it was paid off, so I was looking for neither a new car nor another car payment. He felt like shit, and I supported him feeling like such. That was probably the only time in our relationship when I really wished he had money. I wished he could have bought me a new car. I needed him to buy me a new car. His teaching business was not exactly bringing in a generous salary, and I had just helped him finance a new business venture. I bought the house under my name alone a couple of years earlier because that's the way we had to do it. We had a motorcycle that I also financed because I loved him, and I knew it would make him happy. I had just finished paying off my own engagement ring (yes, I know I shouldn't mention that). Now we just spent more money for our wedding escapade. My reserve was running low, and the economy was deteriorating on an hourly basis (Early 2008).

Punches come in twos, right? Well, a couple days later, my mom had an accident and was hospitalized in Montreal. I drove to Montreal in a snowstorm the same day in the new used car I had just reluctantly bought. Hey, maybe the new car saved my life on some awful roads. I'll never know.

A few months earlier, my mom had been diagnosed with ovarian cancer, and she had a cyst the size of a grapefruit in one of her ovaries that was growing rapidly. Her ovary exploded one day while she was taking the subway home from work; the liquid in the cyst was incredibly acidic, so it damaged all the neighboring organs. The liquid was also full of cancer cells which were scattered all over her abdominal cavity. She now needed six months of chemotherapy to eradicate all the cancer cells.

While tending to my mom in Montreal, I received a call from the family of a woman who owned yet another dance school right down the street from me. She had recently passed away, and they were hoping that I would be able to take over the business so that it remained a dance studio. It felt like another wink from the universe, so I couldn't say no.

Her dance school offered other types of dance instruction than what I was teaching, mainly ballroom and recreational tap and jazz for kids, so we were never in direct competition with each other. Dance classes had been offered there for the last 30 years in a beautiful space that used to be the village's church. Another 30 years earlier, she and her husband transformed the interior of the church into the dance studio it was now, which had a wonderful energy. My studio at the time was in an old warehouse made of steel in which we were able to do great things, but "charming" was not the first impression it made on visitors.

Over the last six years, I acquired two large warehouse bays that housed dance studios, two lobbies for changing rooms and a rest area, and one office in a separate part of the building. We seemed to need more and more space every six months, so we continued to expand anytime an adjacent space became available. It came at the perfect time even though there was so much else going on all at once.

I continued commuting back and forth between Montreal and the Cape for a few months while negotiating the terms of the new agreement. Eventually the business they inherited would be folded into my business, and I would move into the studio in the old church. Meanwhile, my relationship with Brad was changing; I felt I couldn't rely on him as much as I'd hoped I could. My life was getting busier, and I was feeling lonelier.

Knee Surgery

Six years earlier, I had a bad fall on stage in the dress rehearsal for a show I was co-directing. The other director was late, so I was attempting to direct and dance at the same time. The dancing included leaps off chairs that were just painted. Altogether, it was not a good picture. I incorrectly leapt off a chair while trying to correct one of the arm gestures, and before I knew it, I was on the ground swearing in all sorts of languages—English, mostly, since they're my favorites. I left in an ambulance. Because I am a ballerina, and since ballerinas don't tear their anterior cruciate ligaments (ACLs) like football players do, the doctors saw no need for an MRI and sent me home with what they diagnosed as a sprained knee. Six years later and multiple solo performances later, I learned that ever since the accident, I had no ACL or lateral collateral ligament (LCL) in my left knee, which explained the pain I was always in. By the time I was seen by a qualified doctor in Boston, little of both meniscuses was left either. The amount of movement in my knee had ground most of them down. Needless to say, I wasn't happy about this news.

The only reason I was able to perform for those six years was that I had enough muscle strength around my knee to keep it in place. I felt discouraged when I realized I had pushed my body so hard during all those years when in reality, I was badly injured. It made me start to think about the way I was living my life. I am a survivor. I never ask people for much. I rely on myself first and on others only when necessary. It is pretty simple: I wake up and do what needs to be done to make things work.

Having knee surgery was something that needed to be done, and there was no way around it. By the time I did see a good doctor, I had trouble getting through the day without pain - deep, heart-stopping pain.

It felt like I was carrying most of the load financially, so it was an in convenient time to stop teaching to have the surgery; it was also an added emotional stress. I was negotiating the terms of my move into the new studio, I was traveling regularly to see my mom in Canada to help her manage while she was on chemo, and I had a spring recital to produce. But that spring, I was having trouble doing any activity without pain.

I had my spring recital on May 30th. June 1st we were moving in the new studio. I scheduled knee surgery for early August. Hey, why not? I was 31; I could do it. In order to regain full mobility of my knee, I had to stay in the CPM machine for six weeks, and four of those six weeks, I had to be in bed pretty much every hour of the day and night. I ran the business from my bed for four weeks. I was putting a summer production together three weeks after the surgery which I could hardly stand up for. If I remember correctly, I ended m/cing the whole evening on Percocet; it must have been fun for the audience.

Brad and I were also planning a wedding celebration for Columbus Day weekend for our families to meet. I was putting a full-length "Nutcracker" production later in December and started teaching full-time on crutches starting in September. I was still heavily medicated while doing my fall schedule. I even hired some of my new teachers from my living room couch.

I was running a full dance studio with over 18 teachers in a new space. I had no idea how to manage all that staff, and I still had to get my ass into physical therapy every day so that I may, one day, have full use of my leg again. Let's just say that I felt like I was carrying the whole world on my shoulders. Brad seemed to see or appreciate none of it. I started to see a regular therapist on the side (I call it head therapy) to help cope with the situation.

At a time when it would have been nice for my husband to help out, he seemed to find deeper layers of hatred towards me. It was the therapist's opinion at the time that Brad was trying to put me down so I would stay with him. He said if he makes you feel bad enough about yourself, you are going to be too scared to leave him. I was.

My leg was in the CPM machine for so long that I started losing a lot of skin due to the lack of movement and poor circulation. I thought the skin on my foot would all come off. Gross, I know. I don't ask for much, but I did ask my husband to help me clean my foot. I couldn't reach it, and honestly, it was freaking me out. He never accepted to touch, clean, or rub my foot.

Things weren't right. I started to see the situation in a new light. A few weeks before our wedding party, he lashed out and accused me of being hard to work with and that no one in his family would want to help because nothing is ever good enough for me. I see how couples are run around here, and I really think I did the best I could. I had a home-cooked meal on the table most nights, and I really did everything I could to support him. I needed just a little bit of help… or love.

The final straw for me was when Brad announced he was to have knee surgery over the holidays. I must have looked like I was having a good time… I had just barely survived the fall, and now I was supposed to take care of him over the winter. I had always been supportive of him, but I needed him to step up to give me a little break just about then, and now he decided that he was taking the winter off to make himself better. Well, his family came down to help for his surgery. I was busy teaching every class I could to subsidize his income. I was bitter about it. He moved out shortly after recovering from his surgery.

The Separation

When I had my knee surgery, I believed that it would be a good opportunity to contemplate a few things in my life, get myself re-aligned, and possibly make some changes. Specifically, certain changes needed to happen with the dance studio. After the surgery, however, I started to realize that the dance studio, its staff, and the community of people surrounding the studio were there to support me. The business was now strong enough to let me rest up. It was my personal relationship that had become unsatisfactory.

It was a hard realization. I think I would have changed anything about myself to make the relationship work if I could. Leaving Brad was difficult because I felt it put me back where I was when Phillip left nine years earlier. I didn't like it. I didn't like the idea of failing another relationship, but with time, I realized we hadn't. We had had a great relationship until it stopped being great, and then we split up. Brad and I managed to remain friends after some time passed. We did get divorced, but we managed to save our friendship, and that was most important for the both of us.

Getting Back on My Feet

Getting back on my feet after the separation took some time. I was told over and over again: "Give it some time." That's tough advice, but it was still good advice. I now had the chance to really spend time getting to know myself again; I had no idea how disconnected I had become. At first, I didn't even know what I wanted to do with my free time; it's not that I had much of it, but I still didn't know what to do with myself when I wasn't working. And I couldn't just jump into another relationship. I was sore.

It was time for some changes. For one thing, I learned to work less. Even with all the financial responsibility and business resting squarely on my own shoulders, I felt like I had fewer financial obligations after the separation. I worked on restructuring my schedule in a way that worked for me. As a result, I found myself a lot happier. I learned to relax a bit more, let go, and rejoice in the small things that life has to offer.

When I started teaching on Cape Cod my prayer was that my involvement with students would be a positive experience. This defined my teaching philosophies. Over the years, the dance center's mission became that of teaching dance with the care needed to make it a positive experience.

After going through ballet training myself, I was very aware of the positive or negative impact I could have as a teacher on the lives of the young girls and boys in my class. I was very scared - I wasn't sure I was ready for such a responsibility. If I didn't have to support myself, I might have chickened out. I swear, I was physically ill before my first class on the Cape.

At the time, it helped to return to the practice that I learned at the ashram: to offer my work as a selfless service, as work performed without attachment and therefore without ego. As a new teacher, I started to offer my teaching as a spiritual practice, and prayed that my interactions with the students be filled with the light of my intention.

Building self-esteem had become a passion for me at the studio and now that I was faced with the reality of the divorce, I took a long deep breath. I had to find my own self-esteem. I had to find that self, own that self, and love that self. And that is when the Golden Rule really came true for me.

Golden Rule 12
Build Self-Esteem, Not Egos

Differentiating between the two can be a little be tricky at first. A simple way to compare one with the other is like this: self-esteem is how we feel about ourselves, while the ego is how we compare ourselves to others. As dance teachers, we can decide to build self-esteem in a student rather than groom the ego by bringing them back to their own practice and focus back on themself.

It is important to me that my younger dancers know right from the start that everyone has an important part to play. Maybe this time you will be in the front; maybe next time you will be in the back. Both times, your presence is needed whether you are center stage or a part of the scene.

There shouldn't be a hierarchy; we all have a part to play. Just as we shouldn't compare each other when things change or end unexpectedly in life or in a relationship. When someone else has the lead role, they are playing that role because of our support, our kind words, our love, and our presence. I teach my students that trusting that they have exactly what they need is an important part of finding inner happiness. As much as I support their dreams, I also want them to be happy with who they are as they pursue those dreams.

It is important to highlight the success of each one of the dancers because we do need to celebrate achievements in a way that does not take away the other dancer's importance. Sports does well with this understanding. Perhaps it is the nature of team sports, the success of one makes for the success of all players. In dance, I believe there is a way to enforce that as well. Because it is a group practice, we need to encourage support and appreciation of each other's merits. It influences everyone positively.

Self-esteem is close to the ego, but it doesn't have a competitive edge to it. It has an inclusive energy. When students feel good about their training and their achievement in dance or other activities, they will be supportive of others, understanding, and giving. When ego is built, there is tension, conflict, and a lack of acceptance of others.

This is real life. We know it is not always easy to support someone else in their achievement when we feel like ours are less. It makes us feel bad because we compare ourselves. But the truth is that trusting that your turn will come too, that you also have your own strength and successes in your own way, helps to keep our enthusiasm going and keep our hearts moist with loving energy.

Learning to be yourself without the fear of judgment takes courage and a sense of self that is not affected by where others place you in comparison to where they are. Being strong is something we can all help develop in each other and it is something as teachers that we can help build right on the dance floor.

In my words

Chapter 13: L'après-Spectacle [After the Shows]

A New Dawn

One day, after the separation, I woke up with a very stark realization: I could simply stop feeling unworthy of attention and love. It took me years to realize the impact of the feeling of abandonment I experienced from both my parents. A lot of people are raised with a much stronger sense of self-worth than I was. It has taken a lot of work to get to this place in my life where I am willing to stand up for myself.

In a way, it is my love for each one of my students that made me work on strengthening my own sense of self-worth. When I did, and when I took a good look at myself, I realized that it just made sense to stop compromising my own happiness due to my old feelings of loneliness and unworthiness.

I learned in the years after my second separation and divorce that I needed to stand true to who I am. I vowed to stop judging myself so much for things that happened. I blamed myself a lot for many months following my break-up with Brad for not being able to make the relationship work, and yet there were so many elements in my life that were so magical. I had to own what happened, and move on. I had to learn to truly stand up for who I was and commit to it.
The first step in creating change in my personal life was to stop trying so hard to please others. For so long, I'd been afraid of being rejected again, and I tended to please others rather than being truly honest with myself.

Over the years I had gotten used to making sure I would be liked or, at least not judged. I became used to not communicating the way I felt right away, so as not to make waves. This only created bigger waves down the road when things stayed unsaid for so long. I'd become afraid of what would happen if I stopped censoring myself.

I became more willing to talk to people around me about my personal life without fearing they would judge me or think less of me. Writing about my life has certainly helped me process some of my past so that I could more easily talk about it without being vague or emotional. I learned to express my emotions in real time, and it quickly became an exercise in trusting myself and others.

It turned out that opening up and telling people how I was doing, good or bad, helped create situations where conversations could start, and we could somehow bond in a casual greeting.

Learning to express my emotions in real time and in personal situations came from my desire to create healthier relationships with others and to stop the pattern of isolation I had nurtured for so many years, either consciously or unconsciously. I began to understand that another person cannot really get to know me unless I open up.

I was learning to break the walls down, pack the pretense away, and walk forward in life with the vulnerability needed to seek out what my heart really needed. In a way, I started standing straight inside of myself. I started building a real relationship with myself, trusting myself. And this is where this Golden Rule really came to its full meaning for me.

Golden Rule 13
Learn to Stand Straight

The first step in learning to be a dancer is to stand straight; from the first pliés at the barre to the tour à la second in the center, if your shoulders aren't over your ribs, and your ribs are not over your hips, you just won't hold up.

When studying dance, standing straight is the starting point. The beauty of dance training is that students learn to stand straight for the sheer purpose of efficiency, as it is the key to balance, the key to turns, and the key to finding greater extension and strength in the body.

But standing straight goes beyond the posture; it is also a state of being in line with one's self. It is a way of being within ourselves as well. Standing straight within myself, I've learned to speak the truth about what is going on in my life. I've learned to be present with both myself and the situation and to act in a way that respects others while also maintaining my self-respect.

I believe standing straight inside helps us be physically, emotionally, mentally, and energetically in alignment within one's self. In turn, this inner posture helps us pursue our dreams and achieve our goals. It is making sure our actions, our hearts, and our minds work together in harmony.

Being in a dance studio, students learn to conquer their own obstacles whatever they may be: overcoming a physical challenge, fatigue, a sad moment, or anxiety. Standing straight is the best way to align the will with the heart and the heart with the mind.

I want to provide students with a space where they can be themselves, push themselves, and keep asking themselves: "What is it that I really want? What is it that I can really do? How can I better communicate who I really am?" It is building that inner posture that will help them become stronger and more assertive in who they are.

Most students will pursue careers other than dance, but learning to stand straight with their own self and their own voice will continue to support all facets of their lives. Their goals may change, but they'll never stop having goals.

Standing straight is an ongoing conversation with the teenagers in class. They will stand straight at the barre and while they go across the barre, but then they'll go right back to slouching in the corner. I remember one day in class, they really weren't paying attention to what I was talking about when it came to their posture. I was simply saying, "Just keep it up." I was trying to explain how dramatically different it was to stand straight in pretty much everything we do. It should be a state, not just a position that we go in and out of.

For those that teach teenagers, you'll know what I mean when I say I am pretty sure they were listening, but no one was responding. It's amazing how they can all just look at you sometimes and make you feel like they don't speak the same language. So I said here, "I'll show you," and I proceeded to teach the next part of the class by walking around with my knees bent, my back rounded, and my head hunched over just a bit. "You'll see for yourself," I said.

Two minutes later, they were giggling and pleading me to stop. It worked. They stopped. I've not had that conversation ever again. So stand straight. Let's not hide. Let's not make excuses. Be yourself, both internally and externally, because we honor each part of ourselves and want to be true to it.

We need to learn to honor ourselves by owning the life we have, the body we have, the mind we have, and the heart we have and take care of it all because it is our greatest responsibility.

Preparing to go across the floor in class

Chapter 14: La Critique [The Critic]

Self-Acceptance

I have now been living in the United States for over 10 years. During this period, I have spent a lot of time with my family, both here in the United States and in Canada.

For a long time, I felt responsible for the events that occurred in my family from the time I was five until I was 14; I really believed I had done something wrong for my childhood life to unfold this way. I must have behaved in a way that made my parents want to leave me behind, and I thought my circumstances were a reflection of who I was.

I secretly believed if I had been treated as if I didn't deserve to be loved and taken care of, then I certainly must not have deserved to be loved and cared for. It's not completely uncommon to come to an age when we have enough inner strength to look at things again that have just been buried underneath it all. In learning to accept who I am, I started thinking about the meaning of self-acceptance.

Self-acceptance is a harder concept than it seems; it's certainly harder than I thought it would be. Self-acceptance is not meant to be selective. If we think of ourselves as being multifaceted or split up into different parts, I think it is fair to say that some parts are easier to accept than others. Can we accept only the good parts of ourselves and cut some parts out when it comes to self-acceptance? I guess my biggest question when it comes to self-acceptance is this: does self-acceptance mean that I must accept my past?

The love that I feel towards all my students is such that if any one of them ever was in the situation of needing a home, I would welcome him or her into mine - and I have. How can anyone not want to take care of a child? It is incomprehensible to me. I am saying that not as a judgement of my parents but more to express the difficulty I had in accepting my past.

We are so vulnerable when we are young. Despite how much children may misbehave, they always need protection. Despite how challenging they may be, children are never misbehaving with the hope of being abandoned. Their acting out is a scream for help. No one seeks abandonment, and everyone wants to be loved.

Many times, I have held a child who went from screaming and fighting to breaking down into tears and telling me what was really going on. I have often wished that someone had done that for me as a child—to simply let me break down and pour my heart out.

In contemplating self-acceptance I started seeing that there was a part of me that was still angry at the way things had turned out when I was a child. I had a very angry seven-year-old self inside who was still pissed for having been left behind. She was still unsettled, stirring me up, making it very difficult for me to trust myself. And somehow it hit me. Maybe it's not that I had trouble accepting my past, maybe it's that I still hadn't accepted her.

I had been treating my own inner angry self as a child the same way so many people treat wound-up seven-year-olds: I had been ignoring her! It's not the situation that I hadn't accepted; it was my own reaction to it. When she screamed in my face, I would turn my back on her. "Grow up," I'd said to her. "You're too loud and annoying."

Somehow I had to accept her back into my own sacred space. No one else could do that for me now, and no one other than me could really bring her back and comfort her. I had to look at her. I had to make her feel safe. I had to take her back into the temple of my heart. As I gave myself time to validate my experience as a child I saw how much she had hurt. She hurt a lot. There were a lot of emotions I had repressed, there was a lot of anger buried inside.

I remember my last day at the ashram, the summer I was 14. I went back to the temple where I had spent many hours chanting and meditating. Once inside, I remember saying to myself, I am leaving my heart here. I didn't know where I was going, and I had no idea what was going to happen to me. I wanted to leave my heart in this sacred space so it would be safe. But somewhere inside me I heard: Bring the temple into your heart instead.

I remember staying standing there inside the temple for a moment not understanding what had just happened. And then I understood. I had to take the temple with me in my heart. The temple was my heart. My heart was my temple. My temple was my love. That love is my own sacred place.

That sacred place inside was to become my anchor, my roots, and the place I would welcome back my seven year old self and heal her wounds. Self-acceptance has taught me that I am the only person who needs to believe that my experience was true. No one else needs to recognise that what happened to me hurt me. The experience is the truth.

Taking that little girl back in and accepting the challenge to take a look at her wounds allowed me to trust myself in a whole new way. Maybe self-acceptance is not only seeing all the various pieces inside of us but trusting that each piece is worthy of being acknowledged, reconnected to, and loved. Trust is the glue that brings all the pieces back together so we can hold the countless blessings life has to offer. Learning to dwell in that feeling of trust and learning to recreate that state of trust for others is what gave birth to the Golden Rule.

Golden Rule 14
Trust Is the Best Fertilizer

Making a space for my students to express themselves and feel safe to do so is how I aspire to cultivate trust in teaching. In a place where one feels protected and confident, they can safely be themselves. The sacred space I found inside myself expanded to the dance floor, and the safety and the freedom I found on the dance floor became my temple. And that is the space I want to recreate for others.

At the dance studio, the dance floor expands beyond the actual dance room; it is in the lounge area, the dressing room, and the community of people that we keep. It is a space as well as a frame of mind, where you know others won't judge you. You won't be laughed at, and you will not be undermined, ignored, or thought less of under any circumstances.

Connecting with ourselves is not always easy in a world where the demands put on the individual are constant and never-ending. It's important for students to feel free to initiate activities, participate in choreographies, and be creative. Their involvement is what will make it possible for them to truly open up.

Finding our own voice takes time, regular practice, and love. Allowing the students to have a voice gives them a chance to define themselves. We are all able to teach one thing or another, but I think the real gift to students is creating a space where they can discover a better understanding of themselves through the experience that we, as educators, provide for them. We, as instructors, need to be sure to protect the environment created so students feel safe, comfortable, and can remain open.

Encouraging and directing students toward the best they can be takes time and continuity, and it all begins with trust. Building trust will translate into an inner and outer space where students feel at ease to come to be themselves. That experience of trust will grow for a longtime, creating long-lasting roots into one's own experience of self.

That is the gift dance can give when done carefully and with love. So protect the purity of the space you create for yourself and the peoplearound you. Accept your experiences. Accept yourself. Trust your experiences. Trust yourself. Cultivate that love and acceptance of others.We all need a home and we all need a safe space to express who we really are.

curtain call on stage

14 Golden Rules of Teaching

1. Never Assume That Kids Are Dumb

No one likes being told to blindly follow the rules, and children are certainly no exception. Find ways to include information in the teaching—from explaining the origin of a step or the reasons behind certain studio etiquettes—so it is more understandable for the students. Clear explanation is key to really connect with the child's mind. Take the time. Explain, explain, explain, and continue to educate yourself so you never run out of answers. Empower them with the knowledge so they feel connected to the moment, which is now.

2. Movement is Born in Stillness

Cultivating stillness is a simple way to teach students to tune in with themselves. Focus your mind, then let movement be something meaningful filled with something unique, something that exists now in the present: you. Stillness is the key to acquiring control and perfecting many dance moves, knowing when to push and when to hold still. So let students familiarize themselves with what stillness is early on. It will not only give them focus in their work, but it will also give them a connection with themselves that gives real comfort to the soul.

3. Keep Students' Enthusiasm Alive

Enthusiasm is essential to progress. As instructors, we have to be mindful of our interactions with each student so as not to extinguish the student's enthusiasm. Enthusiasm brings us back to our own life-force energy. It is our heart, it is our love, and it defines us. So it is imperative to keep your students' enthusiasm alive. Let them connect with their love for the art form or their activities. Let them be good at it, talk about it, and experience it. Sometimes remembering how excited we got about something just this once is a feeling that will stay with us forever.

4. Let Music Be the Guide

Dance was born from music, and sensitivity to music is essential to dancing well. Implementing dance education with introduction to music is a great way to sensitize the students to the art of music. Focusing back on music brings our attention back to the art, and it's the reason one chooses to dance in the first place, to express ourselves. Focusing back on the music will ensure that dancers focus back on dance as an art form and not their ego.

5. Dance Training Is a Path, Not a Leap

Remind students that dance training is a path and never just one leap. Students should develop and fine tune their skills along that path at their own pace. Seeking specific results in an unrealistic time frame can lead to both physical injury and feelings of inadequacy. Training a dancer takes time and patience. Keep students balanced by offering a curriculum that provides guidance on body alignment, thorough warm-up routines, and strengthening exercises. There are no overnight achievements in dance training, as it all gets built up slowly. The keys to successful dance training are repetition, commitment, and doing it all over again tomorrow.

6. Find Your Own Natural Movement

Dance needs to be filled with the person's real emotions in order to be effective. Encourage dancers to stay in touch with that essence, the emotions, and continue to build their own personal connection to dance. The technique alone does not have expressive values. It is impressive, but in order for a soul to be touched, the other person's soul has to be there, too. Allowing time for students to explore their own natural movement builds the ability to express themselves through dance in a meaningful way.

7. Set Goals

If you don't really know what you are aiming for, it is hard to be successful. By learning to set small, attainable goals, students learn the power of their minds when it comes to surmounting obstacles. Implement goal setting in all aspects of dance teaching, whether it is at the beginning or end of a semester, the beginning or end of a class, or the beginning or end of an across-the-floor exercise. Goal setting centers the mind on the now, where the actions take place. Thoughts move us forward, and emotions move us back; the mind walks us through the now.

8. Competition Should Never Lead to Hatred

Competition is a great way to keep the level of energy high in a class. When we focus our competitiveness on ourselves, we push ourselves to achieve our own goals. Even the smallest remarks, however, can alter someone's sense of safety, so watch that the dance floor remains a place of fairness for everyone to be in. Don't let competition lead to hatred. Remind everyone that respecting everyone for who they are is the righteous way to be in life and on the dance floor.

9. Learn By Teaching Others

Teaching provides dancers the opportunity to enhance their own understanding of the art form. Use the process of teaching as an important step for students to build their self-esteem and strengthen their understanding of dance. Teaching is a way to empower students in realizing how much they have learned and how much they know. Having to communicate with others forces us to really grab on to the knowledge that was inside of us. The circle created by letting students teach in a way that is supported by a curriculum creates growth on many levels.

10. Find Form, Focus, Energy

We need to remind ourselves to build on all three levels: the form applies to the body and finding that neutral ground to start from, while focus comes from the mind being in the present moment, and energy is the self—the vital energy inside each one of us that defines us, keeps us real and expressive, committed to the now. This balance between all three elements is primordial in teaching and in life as well. I believe having all three elements present in our life is a way to find great happiness.

11. Have Discipline

Teach discipline as a way for students to reaffirm their goals; avoid the misconception that discipline is restricting, punishment, or exemption of power. Don't arbitrarily impose rules, and instead help students think of discipline as a decision to make the best out of their lives. Without such a decision, time is lost, energies are depleted, momentum is stalled, and life can career out of control. When the heart knows its purpose and the mind has set its agenda, discipline is everyone's best friend.

12. Build Self-Esteem, Not Egos

Build self-esteem in a student rather than ego by bringing them back to their own practice and focus back on themselves. When students feel confident about their training and their achievement in dance or other activities, they will be supportive of others, understanding, and giving. When ego is built, there is tension, conflict, and a lack of acceptance of others. There shouldn't be a hierarchy; we all have a part to play. Teach students to trust that they have exactly what they need as a way to find inner happiness and keep the enthusiasm going so the heart is moist with loving energy.

13. Learn to Stand Straight

When studying dance, standing straight is the starting point. Doing so, however, goes beyond the posture; it is also a state of being in line within one's self. Teach students to stand straight internally and externally, as a way to honor each part of ourselves and to be true to it. Providing students with a space where they can be themselves helps build that inner posture to help them become stronger and more assertive in who they are.

14. Trust Is the Best Fertilizer

Make space for students to express themselves and feel safe to do so as a way to cultivate trust. Trust is a safe place as well as a frame of mind where one knows others won't judge you, won't be laughed at, you will not be undermined, or ignored or thought less of under any circumstance. We, as instructors, need to protect the environment created so students feel safe, comfortable, and at ease just to be themselves. Building trust will translate into an inner and outer space where students feel at ease to come to be themselves.

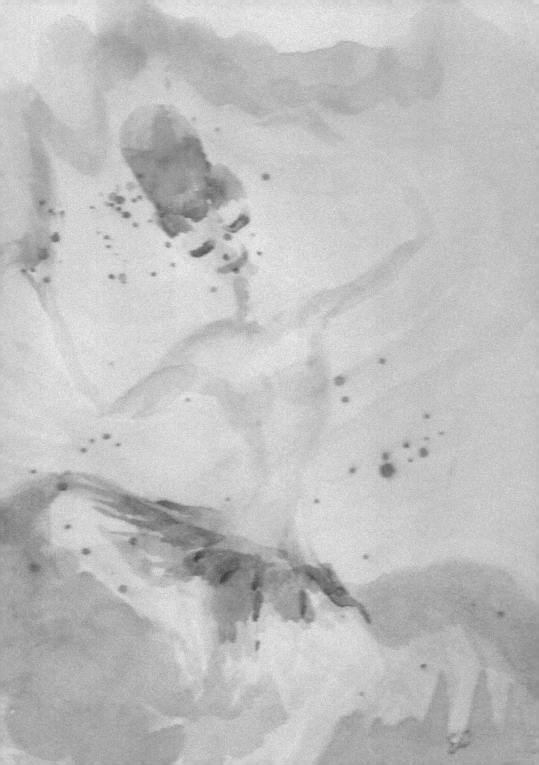

Photo credit:
Cover photo and on page 44, 62, 65, 113, 121: Pascal marchand |
www.pascal-marchand.com

Photo on page 5, 18, 42, 100, 109, 114, 139: Leigh Mohan

Photo on page 36 & backcover: Robert Etcheverry |
www.robertetcheverry.com

Photo on page 52: Felix Lavoie

Photo on page 58, 76, 144: Glenn Pokraka

Photo on page 68, 71, 118: Steve Heaslip | Cape Cod Times File

Photos on page 102: Bob Tucker | FocalPoint Studio|
www.focalpointstudio.com

Photo on page 128: Kate Murphy | KML Photography |
www.kmlphotography.net

Photo on page 8, 11, 14, 24, 29, 39, 46, 59, 74, 78, 83, 87, 91, 93,
96: Family photos or required no credit to the photographer.

Special thanks to Cynthia Buck, Jane E. Caputo, Meghan Carmi-
chael, Sandra Cavallo, Leigh Mohan, Sujata Ringawa, Antonia
Stephens, and Willow Moon Publishing for all your feedback
and guidance.

est difficile pour moi de vous parler de la méditation parce que pour moi
... des expériences tandis que pour vous ça peu rester que de simples
... sur une feuille. Je vais commencer par vous faire part d'une
... servation intéressante que j'ai lu et je vous l'explique du mieux que
... peux dans mes mots: En chacun de nous se trouve d'une façon
... cagée, une lumière qui est appellé aussi notre "Soi". Si nous
... réfléchissons ensuite à toute la joie que nous retirons des activités
... ...tidiennes et des biens matériels accumulés, on s'aperçoit que
... ...te joie on ne la retrouve pas à l'extérieur mais en nous-même,
... ...nd on prend le temps de s'intérioriser et de retrouver notre
... ...mière.

... méditation est cet instant d'intériorisation où on prend
... ...tact avec notre "Soi". Il suffit de se fermer les yeux, ne plus penser
... ...ien de se laisser pénétrer par le silence, devenir attentif à ce
... ...se passe à l'intérieur. On rentre alors dans l'état de prendre
... ...science de ce qui en nous ne change pas, sans faire d'efforts
... ...t un état une façon d'être.

... lu aussi quelque chose que je voudrais vous partager et qui nous
... ...che tous: "les hommes, les hommes normaux vivent dans un état
... ...d'abstration profonde, dans un demi-sommeil constant". Ma façon
... ...comprendre cela est que pour arriver à vivre dans un état
... ...accord parfait, ça prend beaucoup de temps, de purifications,
... ...coute de tous les messages intérieurs.

CPSIA information can be obtained
at www.ICGtesting.com
Printed in the USA
LVHW071947051118
595972LV00023B/662/P

9 781948 256179